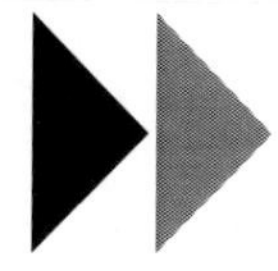

CPCU 555 Course Guide

Personal Risk Management and Property-Casualty Insurance 2nd Edition

The Institutes
720 Providence Road, Suite 100
Malvern, Pennsylvania 19355-3433

Unless otherwise apparent, examples used in The Institutes materials related to this course are based on hypothetical situations and are for educational purposes only. The characters, persons, products, services, and organizations described in these examples are fictional. Any similarity or resemblance to any other character, person, product, services, or organization is merely coincidental. The Institutes are not responsible for such coincidental or accidental resemblances.

This material may contain Internet website links external to The Institutes. The Institutes neither approve nor endorse any information, products, or services to which any external websites refer. Nor do The Institutes control these websites' content or the procedures for website content development.

The Institutes specifically disclaim any implied warranties of merchantability or fitness for a particular purpose. No warranty may be created or extended by sales representatives or written sales materials.

The Institutes materials related to this course are provided with the understanding that The Institutes are not engaged in rendering legal, accounting, or other professional service. Nor are The Institutes explicitly or implicitly stating that any of the processes, procedures, or policies described in the materials are the only appropriate ones to use. The advice and strategies contained herein may not be suitable for every situation.

2nd Edition • 2nd Printing • December 2014

ISBN 978-0-89463-664-6

Contents

Study Materials Available for CPCU 555

Personal Risk Management and Property-Casualty Insurance, 2nd ed., 2013, AICPCU.

CPCU 555 *Course Guide*, 2nd ed., 2013, AICPCU (includes access code for SMART Online Practice Exams).

CPCU 555 SMART Study Aids—Review Notes and Flash Cards, 2nd ed.

The Institutes' Handbook of Insurance Policies, AICPCU.

Student Resources

Catalog A complete listing of our offerings can be found in The Institutes' professional development catalog, including information about:

- Current programs and courses
- Current textbooks, course guides, SMART Study Aids, and online offerings
- Program completion requirements
- Exam registration

To obtain a copy of the catalog, visit our website at www.TheInstitutes.org or contact Customer Service at (800) 644-2101.

How to Prepare for Institutes Exams This free handbook is designed to help you by:

- Giving you ideas on how to use textbooks and course guides as effective learning tools
- Providing steps for answering exam questions effectively
- Recommending exam-day strategies

The handbook is printable from the Student Services Center on The Institutes' website at www.TheInstitutes.org or available by calling Customer Service at (800) 644-2101.

Educational Counseling Services To ensure that you take courses matching both your needs and your skills, you can obtain free counseling from The Institutes by:

- Emailing your questions to advising@TheInstitutes.org
- Calling an Institutes' counselor directly at (610) 644-2100, ext. 7601
- Obtaining and completing a self-inventory form, available on our website at www.TheInstitutes.org or by contacting Customer Service at (800) 644-2101

Exam Registration Information As you proceed with your studies, be sure to arrange for your exam.

- Visit our website at www.TheInstitutes.org/forms to access and print the Registration Booklet, which contains information and forms needed to register for your exam.
- Plan to register with The Institutes well in advance of your exam.

How to Contact The Institutes For more information on any of these publications and services:

- Visit our website at www.TheInstitutes.org
- Call us at (800) 644-2101 or (610) 644-2100 outside the U.S.
- Email us at customerservice@TheInstitutes.org
- Fax us at (610) 640-9576
- Write to us at The Institutes, Customer Service, 720 Providence Road, Suite 100, Malvern, PA 19355-3433

Using This Course Guide

This course guide will help you learn the course content and prepare for the exam.

Each assignment in this course guide typically includes the following components:

Educational Objectives These are the most important study tools in the course guide. Because all of the questions on the exam are based on the Educational Objectives, the best way to study for the exam is to focus on these objectives.

Each Educational Objective typically begins with one of the following action words, which indicate the level of understanding required for the exam:

Analyze—Determine the nature and the relationship of the parts.

Apply—Put to use for a practical purpose.

Associate—Bring together into relationship.

Calculate—Determine numeric values by mathematical process.

Classify—Arrange or organize according to class or category.

Compare—Show similarities and differences.

Contrast—Show only differences.

Define—Give a clear, concise meaning.

Describe—Represent or give an account.

Determine—Settle or decide.

Evaluate—Determine the value or merit.

Explain—Relate the importance or application.

Identify or list—Name or make a list.

Illustrate—Give an example.

Justify—Show to be right or reasonable.

Paraphrase—Restate in your own words.

Recommend—Suggest or endorse something to be used.

Summarize—Concisely state the main points.

Outline The outline lists the topics in the assignment. Read the outline before the required reading to become familiar with the assignment content and the relationships of topics.

Key Words and Phrases These words and phrases are fundamental to understanding the assignment and have a common meaning for those working in insurance. After completing the required reading, test your understanding of the assignment's Key Words and Phrases by writing their definitions.

Review Questions The review questions test your understanding of what you have read. Review the Educational Objectives and required reading, then answer the questions to the best of your ability. When you are finished, check the answers at the end of the assignment to evaluate your comprehension.

Application Questions These questions continue to test your knowledge of the required reading by applying what you've studied to "hypothetical" real-life situations. Again, check the suggested answers at the end of the assignment to review your progress.

Sample Exam Your course guide includes a sample exam (located at the back) or a code for accessing SMART Online Practice Exams (which appears on the inside of the cover). Use the option available for the course you're taking to become familiar with the test format.

For courses that offer SMART Online Practice Exams, you can either download and print a sample credentialing exam or take full practice exams using questions like those that will appear on your credentialing exam. SMART Online Practice Exams are as close as you can get to experiencing an actual exam before taking one.

More Study Aids

The Institutes also produce supplemental study tools, called SMART Study Aids, for many of our courses. When SMART Study Aids are available for a course, they are listed on page iii of the course guide. SMART Study Aids include Review Notes and Flash Cards and are excellent tools to help you learn and retain the information in each assignment.

Direct Your Learning 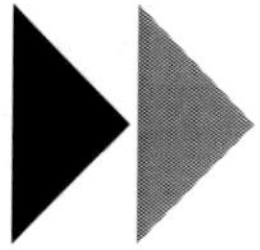

1

Personal Risk Management

Educational Objectives

After learning the content of this assignment, you should be able to:

1. Describe the property loss exposures that individuals and families might face in terms of each of the following:
   - The assets exposed to loss
   - The causes of loss
   - The financial consequences of loss
2. Describe the liability loss exposures that individuals and families might face in terms of each of the following:
   - The assets exposed to loss
   - The causes of loss
   - The financial consequences of loss
3. Demonstrate how the six steps of the risk management process can guide individuals and families in their risk management decisions.
4. Describe how risk control and risk financing techniques are used by individuals and families.
5. Given a scenario regarding an individual or a family's property and liability loss exposures, evaluate the loss exposures and recommend an appropriate risk management technique for each.

Outline

- **Property Loss Exposures**
  - A. Assets Exposed to Loss
    - 1. Real Property
    - 2. Personal Property
  - B. Causes of Loss
  - C. Financial Consequences of Loss
- **Liability Loss Exposures**
  - A. Assets Exposed to Loss
  - B. Causes of Loss
    - 1. Tort Liability
    - 2. Contractual Liability
    - 3. Statutory Liability
  - C. Financial Consequences of Loss
- **Risk Management Process**
  - A. Step 1: Identifying Loss Exposures
  - B. Step 2: Analyzing Loss Exposures
  - C. Step 3: Examining the Feasibility of Risk Management Techniques
  - D. Step 4: Selecting the Appropriate Risk Management Techniques
  - E. Step 5: Implementing the Selected Risk Management Techniques
  - F. Step 6: Monitoring Results and Revising the Risk Management Program
- **Risk Management Techniques**
  - A. Risk Control Techniques
    - 1. Avoidance
    - 2. Loss Prevention
    - 3. Loss Reduction
    - 4. Separation
    - 5. Duplication
    - 6. Diversification
  - B. Risk Financing Techniques
    - 1. Retention
    - 2. Transfer
- **Personal Risk Management Case Study**
  - A. Case Facts
  - B. Case Analysis Tools and Information
  - C. Case Analysis Steps
    - 1. Identify and Analyze Property and Liability Loss Exposures
    - 2. Examine Feasible Risk Management Techniques
    - 3. Select the Appropriate Risk Management Techniques
    - 4. Implement the Risk Management Plans and Monitor the Results

s.m.a.r.t.® tips Don't spend time on material you have already mastered. The SMART Review Notes are organized by the Educational Objectives found in each assignment to help you track your study.

For each assignment, you should define or describe each of the Key Words and Phrases and answer each of the Review and Application Questions.

Educational Objective 1

Describe the property loss exposures that individuals and families might face in terms of each of the following:

- **The assets exposed to loss**
- **The causes of loss**
- **The financial consequences of loss**

Key Words and Phrases

Property loss exposure

Real property (realty)

Personal property

Review Questions

1-1. What is a property loss exposure?

1-2. Individuals and families may own assets that are exposed to loss. Assets are any items of property that have value.

a. What are two types of property that individuals and families own that may be exposed to loss?

b. For your answers to (a), provide an example for each.

1-3. Name some causes of loss that might damage or destroy a dwelling.

1-4. What are three financial consequences of loss?

Application Question

1-5. Virtually all individuals and families have property loss exposures. Assume a family owns a fully furnished home that includes a yard, storage shed, and several fruit trees.

a. What are the assets exposed to loss that the family might have as a consequence of home ownership?

b. What are the causes of loss the family might face as a consequence of home ownership?

c. What are the financial consequences of loss the family might face arising from home ownership?

Educational Objective 2

Describe the liability loss exposures that individuals and families might face in terms of each of the following:

- **The assets exposed to loss**
- **The causes of loss**
- **The financial consequences of loss**

Key Words and Phrases

Liability loss exposure

Damages

General damages

Special damages

Punitive damages (exemplary damages)

Civil law

Tort

Negligence

Review Questions

2-1. Identify the assets exposed to loss in a liability loss exposure.

2-2. Identify the cause of loss associated with a liability loss exposure.

2-3. Describe the financial consequences of a liability loss exposure.

2-4. Identify the four elements of negligence.

2-5. Identify four examples of intentional torts.

Application Question

2-6. Sean has a disagreement with his neighbor, John, and physically harms him, causing John to be admitted to the hospital. John subsequently files a lawsuit against Sean.

a. Which of Sean's assets are exposed to loss?

b. What is the cause of Sean's loss?

c. What are the potential financial consequences for Sean?

Educational Objective 3

Demonstrate how the six steps of the risk management process can guide individuals and families in their risk management decisions.

Key Words and Phrases

Risk management process

Risk control

Risk financing

Review Questions

3-1. List the six steps of the risk management process.

3-2. Describe the loss characteristics that individuals and families may use to analyze their loss exposures.

3-3. Describe examples of measures that individuals and families might use to implement the selected risk management techniques.

Application Question

3-4. A family plans to analyze its automobile loss exposures. The mother and father each drive an older-model car. Their three daughters live with them and regularly use their cars in the evenings. Over the last three years, the family has been involved in four minor auto accidents. How might the family use the four dimensions of a loss exposure to analyze its automobile loss exposures?

Educational Objective 4

Describe how risk control and risk financing techniques are used by individuals and families.

Key Words and Phrases

Avoidance

Loss prevention

Loss reduction

Separation

Duplication

Diversification

Retention

Insurance

Transfer

Review Questions

4-1. Identify the risk control techniques used by individuals and families.

4-2. Identify the risk financing techniques used by individuals and families.

4-3. Describe two noninsurance risk transfer techniques.

4-4. Compare loss prevention to loss reduction.

4-5. Contrast planned retention with unplanned retention.

Application Question

4-6. For each of these sets of frequency-severity characteristics, explain whether you would retain or transfer a personal loss exposure with those characteristics:

a. Low severity and low frequency

b. High severity and low frequency

▶▶

c. Low severity and high frequency

d. Medium severity and medium frequency

Educational Objective 5

Given a scenario regarding an individual or a family's property and liability loss exposures, evaluate the loss exposures and recommend an appropriate risk management technique for each.

Key Words and Phrases

Loss control

Hold-harmless agreement (or indemnity agreement)

Application Questions

5-1. The Smith family, which consists of two parents and a one-year-old son, recently moved into a single home that includes a two-car garage, a garden shed, and a swimming pool. Their parents and their insurance agent counseled them that this is an important event in their lives and that, as new homeowners, they should make a conscious effort to use a structured risk management process to assess their loss exposures and develop and implement a risk management plan to manage them. They decide to undertake this project.

a. Outline the steps the Smiths should follow in developing and implementing a risk management plan.

b. What kinds of assets should the Smiths be identifying that are at possible risk of loss?

c. What kinds of loss exposures can affect real and personal property?

d. How would the insurance agent explain to the Smiths that they may be exposed to liability losses?

e. Explain the difference between a loss prevention technique and a loss reduction technique.

f. Explain two types of risk financing techniques.

5-2. For each of the specified assets and loss exposures identified by the Smiths, identify a risk management technique and a specific technique to apply.

Asset	Loss Exposure	Risk Management Technique and Action
Home and shed	Property losses from fire, lightning, windstorm	
Land, home, pool	Liability losses from injury to others while on premises	
Personal property, furniture, clothes, jewelry	Property losses from fire, lightning, windstorm, theft	
Cars	Property losses from an accident Liability losses from injury to others	

Answers to Assignment 1 Questions

NOTE: These answers are provided to give students a basic understanding of acceptable types of responses. They often are not the only valid answers and are not intended to provide an exhaustive response to the questions.

Educational Objective 1

1-1. A property loss exposure is any condition or situation that presents the possibility of a property loss.

1-2. These answers address questions regarding the assets owned by individuals and families:

a. Two types of property that individuals and families own that may be exposed to loss are (1) real property and (2) personal property.

b. (1) Examples of real property that may be exposed to loss can include a home, foundations, underground pipes, sheds attached to the land, or anything growing on the land, including trees. (Other real property examples are acceptable.)

(2) Examples of personal property that may be exposed to loss can include furniture; televisions; electronic equipment, including computers; and additional household personal property, such as appliances, dishes, carpets, sports equipment, clothing, tools, books, jewelry, cameras, and digital recording devices. Other examples of personal property that may be exposed to loss can include autos, boats, and intangible property. (Other personal property examples are acceptable.)

1-3. Causes of loss (or perils) that can damage or destroy real property, such as a dwelling, include fire, lightning, earthquake, or wind. (Other real property/dwelling cause of loss examples are acceptable.)

1-4. Financial consequences of loss can include one or more of these outcomes:

- Reduction in value of property—the difference between the value of the property before the loss (pre-loss value) and after the loss (post-loss value).
- Increased expenses—expenses in addition to normal living expenses that are necessary because of the loss.
- Lost income—loss of income that results if property is damaged.

1-5. These answers address questions regarding the property loss exposures of individuals and families:

a. Assets exposed to loss include real property and personal property. Real property can include the family's home, foundation, any underground pipes, the storage shed, the land, and the fruit trees. Personal property is all property other than real property, including all the furnishings (or contents) of the home. Such household furnishings for the family might include furniture, carpets, electronics, dishware, clothing, appliances, and numerous other items. (Other real property and personal property examples are acceptable).

b. Causes of loss damage or destroy both real and personal property. As a consequence of home ownership, the family might face such causes of loss affecting their dwelling and furnishings as fire, lightning, earthquake, or wind. (Other causes of loss examples are acceptable).

c. Financial consequences of loss the family might face arising from home ownership include one or more of these outcomes:

 - Reduction in value to the home and furnishings—If a loss occurs, the value of the home and its contents may be less after the loss than it was worth before the loss.
 - Increased expenses—If a loss occurs to the home and its furnishings, the family may face increased living expenses (such as the cost of hotel room rental) in addition to normal living expenses.
 - Lost income—If a loss occurs, in some instances, the family may suffer loss of income as a result of the property damage.

Educational Objective 2

2-1. The assets exposed to loss in a liability loss exposure are money or other financial assets.

2-2. The cause of loss associated with a liability loss exposure is the claim of liability or the filing of a lawsuit.

2-3. The financial consequences of a liability loss exposure are that an individual or a family may lose money or other financial assets. For example, they may have to pay to investigate and defend against the liability claim. Also, a court may award monetary damages if the defense of the claim is not successful or if the claim is settled out of court.

2-4. These are the four elements of negligence:

- A duty to act.
- A breach of that duty.
- An injury or damage occurs.
- The breach of duty is a direct cause of the injury or damage in an unbroken chain of events.

2-5. These are examples of intentional torts:

- Libel
- Slander
- Assault
- Battery
- Trespass
- Nuisance

2-6. These answers address questions regarding John's lawsuit against Sean.

a. The assets exposed to loss are Sean's money and other financial assets.

b. The cause of loss for Sean is the lawsuit filed by John.

c. Sean may need to pay general, special, and punitive damages as a result of the liability suit.

Educational Objective 3

3-1. These are the six steps of the risk management process:

a. Identify loss exposures
b. Analyze loss exposures
c. Examine the feasibility of risk management techniques
d. Select the appropriate risk management techniques
e. Implement the selected risk management techniques
f. Monitor results and revise the risk management program

3-2. The loss characteristics that individuals and families may use to analyze their loss exposures are loss frequency, loss severity, total dollar losses, and timing of losses.

3-3. These are examples of measures individuals and families may use to implement selected risk management techniques:

- Purchasing loss reduction devices
- Contracting for loss prevention services
- Implementing loss control programs
- Obtaining expert advice on how to deal with challenging loss exposures
- Obtaining insurance policies for loss exposures they are not willing to retain
- Creating a list of possessions that may be subject to loss

3-4. The family might analyze its automobile loss exposures in this manner:

- First, it analyzes loss frequency. Four accidents over the last three years are a concern.
- Next, it analyzes loss severity. All four accidents were minor. Perhaps the family would consider maintaining higher collision deductibles on the two older-model cars. The family might retain the cost of minor accidents to avoid increased insurance premiums.
- It would then analyze total dollar losses. The four accidents were minor. However, the family should maintain high liability limits in case any of its members are subsequently involved in a serious auto accident. Even if one of the older cars has to be replaced instead of repaired, the cost of a new vehicle could be covered by family savings.
- Finally, it would analyze the timing of the accidents. Damage from the four accidents was easily repaired. However, the family still should account for the possibility of a future severe liability claim that may cost millions of dollars.

Educational Objective 4

4-1. The risk control techniques individuals and families use include these:

- Avoidance
- Loss prevention
- Loss reduction
- Separation
- Duplication
- Diversification

4-2. The risk financing techniques individuals and families use include these:

- Retention
- Transfer

4-3. A hold-harmless agreement is a noninsurance risk transfer in which one party assumes the legal liability of another party to the contract, such as in an apartment lease. Hedging is another noninsurance risk transfer technique whereby one asset (money) is paid to offset the risk associated with another asset.

4-4. Loss prevention is a risk control technique that reduces the frequency of a particular loss, while loss reduction is a risk control technique that reduces the severity of a particular loss.

4-5. Planned retention is a deliberate assumption of loss that has been identified and analyzed. Unplanned retention is the inadvertent, unplanned assumption of a loss exposure that has not been identified or accurately analyzed.

4-6. These answers address questions regarding frequency-severity characteristics:

a. Losses of low severity and low frequency are predictable and are usually of little financial consequence. These types of losses should be retained.

b. Costs of losses of high severity and low frequency are unpredictable, and they present a high risk. These types of losses would likely be transferred before they occur.

c. Losses of low severity and high frequency are predictable. These types of losses should be retained.

d. Loss exposures of medium severity and medium frequency may be retained or transferred, depending on tolerance for risk and the cost of the risk transfer.

Educational Objective 5

5-1. These answers address questions regarding the Smith family:

a. These are the steps in the risk management process:

- Identify the loss exposures, both property and liability.
- Analyze the loss exposures, considering the potential causes of loss, loss frequency, loss severity, total dollar losses, and timing.
- Examine the feasibility of risk management techniques—that is, actions they can take to reduce frequency or severity of losses—and ways they can finance the costs of loss.
- Select appropriate risk management techniques for the identified property and liability exposures.
- Implement the selected risk management techniques.
- Monitor the results and revise the risk management techniques.

b. They should identify real property and personal property.

c. Fire, windstorm, lightning, theft, and flood can affect real and personal property. Others are possible.

d. Individuals and families may be responsible for injuries they cause to other persons. The costs of injuries to others may result in financial damages or costs of investigation and defense, thus threatening the Smiths with loss of money or other financial assets.

e. A loss prevention technique attempts to prevent a loss from occurring, whereas a loss reduction technique attempts to limit the severity of a loss when it occurs.

f. The two types of risk financing techniques are transfer and retention:

- Insurance transfers the financial consequences of a loss from the insured to the insurer.
- Retention is a technique under which the individual or family pays for losses themselves rather than transferring the financial costs to someone else.

5-2. Applying risk management techniques to these loss exposures and assets could follow these suggestions:

Asset	Loss Exposure	Risk Management Technique and Action
Home and shed	Property losses from fire, lightning, windstorm	Loss prevention: install smoke detectors Loss reduction: provide fire extinguishers Risk financing: retention of small losses; insurance
Land, home, pool	Liability losses from injury to others while on premises	Loss prevention: fence around pool area Risk financing: insurance
Personal property, furniture, clothes, jewelry	Property losses from fire, lightning, windstorm, theft	Loss prevention: smoke detectors, fire proof safe Loss reduction: fire extinguishers Risk financing: insurance
Cars	Property losses from an accident Liability losses from injury to others	Risk financing: retention of small losses; insurance Risk financing: insurance

Direct Your Learning 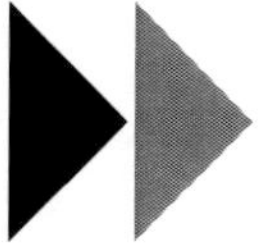

2

The Personal Automobile Insurance Environment

Educational Objectives

After learning the content of this assignment, you should be able to:

1. Evaluate each of the following approaches to compensating automobile accident victims:
    - Tort liability system
    - Financial responsibility laws
    - Compulsory insurance laws
    - Uninsured motorists coverage
    - Underinsured motorists coverage
    - No-fault insurance
2. Describe no-fault automobile laws in terms of each of the following:
    - Types of no-fault laws
    - Benefits required by no-fault laws
3. Explain how high-risk drivers may obtain auto insurance.
4. Describe automobile insurance rate regulation in terms of each of the following:
    - Rating factors
    - Matching price to exposure
    - Competition
    - Other regulatory issues

Outline

- **Compensation of Auto Accident Victims**
  - A. Tort Liability System
  - B. Financial Responsibility Laws
  - C. Compulsory Auto Insurance Laws
  - D. Uninsured Motorists Coverage
  - E. Underinsured Motorists Coverage
  - F. No-Fault Automobile Insurance
- **No-Fault Automobile Laws**
  - A. Types of No-Fault Laws
    - 1. Modified No-Fault Plans
    - 2. Add-On Plans
    - 3. Choice No-Fault Plans
  - B. Benefits Required by No-Fault Laws
- **Automobile Insurance for High-Risk Drivers**
  - A. Voluntary Market Programs
  - B. Residual Market Programs
    - 1. Automobile Insurance Plans
    - 2. Joint Underwriting Associations (JUAs)
    - 3. Other Programs
- **Automobile Insurance Rate Regulation**
  - A. Rating Factors
    - 1. Primary Rating Factors
    - 2. Other Rating Factors
    - 3. Other Discounts and Credits
  - B. Matching Price to Exposure
  - C. Competition
  - D. Other Regulatory Issues
    - 1. Rising Healthcare Costs
    - 2. Environmental Issues
    - 3. Vehicle Modifications

Reduce the number of Key Words and Phrases that you must review. SMART Flash Cards contain the Key Words and Phrases and their definitions, allowing you to set aside those cards that you have mastered.

For each assignment, you should define or describe each of the Key Words and Phrases and answer each of the Review and Application Questions.

Educational Objective 1

Evaluate each of the following approaches to compensating automobile accident victims:

- **Tort liability system**
- **Financial responsibility laws**
- **Compulsory insurance laws**
- **Uninsured motorists coverage**
- **Underinsured motorists coverage**
- **No-fault insurance**

Key Words and Phrases

Financial responsibility law

Compulsory auto insurance law

First party

Unsatisfied judgment fund

Uninsured motorists (UM) coverage

Underinsured motorists (UIM) coverage

No-fault automobile insurance

Review Questions

1-1. Briefly describe how the tort liability system compensates injured auto accident victims.

1-2. Describe three circumstances under which a motorist is required to provide proof of financial responsibility to comply with financial responsibility laws.

1-3. Describe the disadvantages of financial responsibility laws.

1-4. Describe an advantage of compulsory insurance laws, as compared to financial responsibility laws.

1-5. Explain how low-cost auto insurance addresses the problem of uninsured drivers.

1-6. Describe the common characteristics of unsatisfied judgment funds.

1-7. Briefly describe how no-fault automobile insurance operates.

1-8. Explain why no-fault auto insurance laws were developed.

Application Question

1-9. Contrast uninsured motorists coverage (UM) with underinsured motorists coverage (UIM).

Educational Objective 2

Describe no-fault automobile laws in terms of each of the following:

- **Types of no-fault laws**
- **Benefits required by no-fault laws**

Key Words and Phrases

No-fault laws

Monetary threshold (dollar threshold)

Verbal threshold

Add-on plan

Choice no-fault plan

Personal injury protection (PIP) coverage

Subrogation

Review Questions

2-1. Contrast a pure no-fault system with modified no-fault plans.

2-2. Explain how add-on plans differ from choice no-fault plans.

2-3. Identify four benefits required by no-fault laws.

2-4. Describe what determines the personal injury protection (PIP) coverage benefits that insurers provide.

Application Question

2-5. Tom lives in a modified no-fault state and carries the minimum PIP medical coverage limit of $20,000 set by the plan. Tom's state has a monetary threshold for noneconomic losses of $50,000. He sustains injuries in an auto accident and incurs $30,000 in economic losses. Tom also suffers $15,000 in noneconomic losses.

a. What amount of economic losses would Tom collect from his own insurer?

b. What amount of noneconomic losses would Tom collect from his own insurer?

c. Can Tom sue the at-fault party for economic losses in this case? Explain your answer.

d. Can Tom sue the at-fault party for noneconomic losses in this case? Explain your answer.

Educational Objective 3

Explain how high-risk drivers may obtain auto insurance.

Key Words and Phrases

Residual market

Safe driver insurance plan (SDIP)

Automobile insurance plan

Joint underwriting association (JUA)

Reinsurance facility

Review Questions

3-1. Identify two types of programs that provide automobile insurance for high-risk drivers.

3-2. How do the activities of insurers of high-risk drivers in the voluntary market differ from the activities of insurers in the residual market?

3-3. Under a state automobile insurance plan, how are the high-risk drivers apportioned to the auto insurers in that state?

3-4. What roles does a state joint underwriting association (JUA) serve with regard to rates, policy forms, and claim settlement for high-risk drivers?

Application Question

3-5. XYZ Auto Insurance sells insurance in a state that has a reinsurance facility for high-risk drivers. Mary is a high-risk driver who has obtained insurance from XYZ. XYZ, in turn, assigned Mary to the reinsurance facility. Mary subsequently had an auto accident and is responsible for the damage to Bill's auto and for Bill's injuries.

a. Does XYZ or the reinsurance facility accept Mary's application and service her policy?

▶▶

b. Does XYZ or the reinsurance facility handle Bill's liability claim?

c. What organization(s) bears any underwriting losses that result from Bill's liability claim?

Educational Objective 4

Describe automobile insurance rate regulation in terms of each of the following:

- **Rating factors**
- **Matching price to exposure**
- **Competition**
- **Other regulatory issues**

Review Questions

4-1. Explain these automobile insurance rating factors and why insurers use them:

a. Territory

b. Age

c. Driver education

d. Multi-car policy

e. Credit-based insurance score

4-2. Describe the homogeneous classes, or rating categories, that insurers often use to help match price to exposure.

4-3. Explain the relationship between competition and regulatory monitoring of insurance rates and how that monitoring is accomplished.

Application Question

4-4. XYZ Insurance has its home office in a state with a population that consists predominantly of people of a particular ethnic origin. XYZ wanted to encourage state residents to buy insurance policies, so it filed rates with the state insurance regulators that extended a flat 70 percent discount to all applicants of the predominant ethnic origin, after considering other rating factors. Explain why the state regulators might not approve these rates based on each of the following rating objectives.

a. Rates must be adequate to pay all claims and expenses.

b. Rates must not be unfairly discriminatory.

Answers to Assignment 2 Questions

NOTE: These answers are provided to give students a basic understanding of acceptable types of responses. They often are not the only valid answers and are not intended to provide an exhaustive response to the questions.

Educational Objective 1

1-1. If a driver operates an auto in a negligent manner that results in bodily injury to another person or in damage to another's property, the operator can be held legally liable for damages incurred by the injured person. Under the tort liability system, injured auto accident victims must prove that another party was at fault before they can collect damages from that party.

1-2. A motorist is required to provide proof of financial responsibility under these circumstances:

- After an auto accident involving bodily injury or property damage exceeding a certain dollar amount
- After a conviction for certain serious offenses, such as drunk driving or reckless driving, or after losing a driver's license because of repeated violations
- Upon failure to pay a final judgment that results from an auto accident

1-3. These are disadvantages of financial responsibility laws:

- Most financial responsibility requirements become effective only after an accident, a conviction, or a judgment.
- Financial responsibility laws do not guarantee payment to all accident victims. Persons injured by uninsured drivers, hit-and-run drivers, or drivers of stolen cars might not be compensated.
- Injured persons might not be fully indemnified for their injuries even when injured by motorists who can prove financial responsibility. Most financial responsibility laws set minimum financial requirements, which may not fully compensate a victim.

1-4. An advantage of compulsory insurance laws, as compared to financial responsibility laws, is that motorists must provide proof of financial responsibility before an accident occurs. By requiring proof of financial responsibility prior to an accident, compulsory insurance laws go beyond financial responsibility laws by ensuring that accident victims are compensated for their losses.

1-5. Low-cost auto insurance is intended to decrease the number of uninsured drivers by making minimal liability coverage available at a reduced cost. Low-cost insurance programs are intended to provide some level of protection at a reduced cost to assist lower-income drivers in purchasing the insurance coverage required to comply with compulsory auto insurance laws.

1-6. Unsatisfied judgment funds have these characteristics:

- An injured person can receive compensation from the fund after having obtained a judgment against a negligent driver and proving that the judgment cannot be collected.
- The maximum amount paid is generally limited to the state's minimum compulsory insurance requirement. In addition, most funds reduce the amount paid by any amount the injured person has collected from other collateral sources of recovery, such as workers compensation benefits or insurance.
- The negligent driver is not relieved of legal liability when the unsatisfied judgment fund compensates the insured person. The negligent driver's license is revoked until the driver reimburses the fund.

1-7. Under a no-fault system, an injured person does not need to establish fault and prove negligence in order to collect payment for damages. In addition, certain no-fault laws place some restrictions on an injured person's right to sue a negligent driver who causes an accident. In some states, when a claim is below a certain monetary threshold, the injured motorist collects for injuries under his or her own insurance policy.

1-8. No-fault laws were developed to avoid the costly and time-consuming process of determining legal liability for auto accidents under the tort liability system. By eliminating the need to prove fault, no-fault laws allow accident victims to receive benefits much sooner after an accident and, as a result, may allow for a quicker recovery from injuries.

1-9. UM coverage compensates an insured for bodily injury caused by an uninsured motorist, a hit-and-run driver, or a driver whose insurer is insolvent. UIM coverage, on the other hand, provides additional limits of protection to the victim of an auto accident when the negligent driver's insurance limits are insufficient to pay for the damages.

Educational Objective 2

2-1. In a pure no-fault system, injured persons would not need to establish fault or prove negligence to collect payment for damages, but they also would not be able to seek damages through the tort liability system. In contrast, under a modified no-fault plan, injured persons would collect economic losses from their own insurers based on state-mandated PIP benefits, and they can sue at-fault drivers for any economic losses that exceed the no-fault coverage limits.

2-2. An add-on plan allows injured drivers the option of collecting for economic losses through their own insurer, but it places no restrictions on their right to sue a negligent party for damages. In contrast, a choice no-fault plan enables the insured to choose whether to be covered on a modified no-fault basis at the time the policy is purchased or renewed. Under a choice plan, insureds who choose the modified no-fault option have limitations on the right to sue for certain types of auto injuries. Insureds who do not choose the modified no-fault option retain full rights to seek compensation from the negligent party, but they pay a higher premium than those insureds who choose the modified no-fault option.

2-3. Benefits required by no-fault laws include these:

- Medical expenses
- Rehabilitation expenses
- Loss of earnings
- Expenses for essential services
- Funeral expenses
- Survivors' loss benefits

2-4. PIP benefits are determined by state no-fault laws.

2-5. These answers address questions regarding Tom's auto accident:

a. Tom would collect $20,000 in economic losses from his own insurer because his PIP medical coverage is limited to $20,000 and his economic losses ($30,000) exceed the limit.

b. Under modified no-fault laws, insureds cannot collect for noneconomic losses through their PIP coverage, so Tom cannot collect from his insurer for his noneconomic losses.

c. Tom can sue the at-fault party for his economic losses that exceed the $20,000 paid by his insurer—the additional $10,000. To recover any additional losses, he must first prove that the other driver was at fault for the accident.

d. Because Tom's economic losses ($30,000) are below the $50,000 monetary threshold in this modified no-fault state, he cannot sue the at-fault party for his noneconomic losses.

Educational Objective 3

3-1. Two types of programs that provide automobile insurance for high-risk drivers are voluntary market programs and residual market programs.

3-2. Insurers of high-risk drivers in the voluntary market accept their own applications, service their policies, pay their claims and expenses, and retain full responsibility for their own underwriting results. Insurers of high-risk drivers in the residual market may accept applications and service policies, but responsibility for underwriting results is usually transferred to a pool or shared proportionally by all insurers in the market in one of several ways.

3-3. Under a state automobile insurance plan, all auto insurers doing business in the state are assigned their proportionate share of high-risk drivers based on the total volume of auto insurance written in the state.

3-4. The state JUA sets the insurance rates and approves the policy forms to be used for high-risk drivers. The JUA designates servicing insurers that settle claims of high-risk drivers.

3-5. These answers address questions regarding XYZ Auto Insurance.

a. XYZ accepts Mary's application and services her policy.

b. In servicing Mary's policy under the pool arrangement of the reinsurance facility, XYZ handles Bill's liability claim.

c. Because the state has a reinsurance facility, all private insurers doing business in the state share any underwriting losses that occur as a result of Bill's claim.

Educational Objective 4

4-1. These answers address questions regarding automobile insurance rating factors and why insurers use them:

a. Territorial factors include the location where the auto is used and garaged, road conditions, state safety laws, and the extent of traffic regulation. These factors affect the frequency and/or severity of loss.

b. Young drivers have less driving experience and tend to be involved in accidents more frequently than older drivers. Therefore, rates for younger drivers are often higher than those for more experienced drivers.

c. Young drivers who complete an approved driver education course (usually including road experience) often qualify for a premium discount. Drivers age fifty-five and older sometimes qualify for a premium discount for successfully completing defensive driver training courses. Driver training can help reduce the frequency and severity of auto losses.

d. A discount is often given to policyholders who have more than one auto under the same policy. Two or more autos owned by the same insured are usually not driven as often as a single auto. It is less costly for the insurer to cover additional autos under the same contract, so savings may be passed to the insured.

e. This numerical ranking is based on the individual's financial history (similar to a credit score, but without income data) and is sometimes used to determine insurance rates. Research shows that insureds with low insurance scores submit more claims than insureds with high scores.

4-2. Insurers often divide auto insurance applicants into homogeneous classes (rating categories), such as "preferred," "standard," and "nonstandard," that reflect different levels of exposure to loss. Applicants who have good driving records and rating factors present minimal loss exposure and are categorized as preferred. Conversely, applicants who have poor driving records or rating factors present greater loss exposure and are categorized as nonstandard and charged higher rates.

4-3. Intense competition among insurers prompts regulators to monitor rates carefully to ensure adequacy and reasonableness. Regulators monitor rates primarily through insurers' rate filings.

4-4. These answers address questions regarding XYZ Insurance:

a. If a large number of applicants of the predominant ethnic origin had poor driving experience and/or numerous claims, a 70 percent discount on their rate would be unlikely to provide enough profit for the insurer to adequately pay its claims and expenses.

b. A 70 percent discount on rates based on the applicant's ethnic origin is unfairly discriminatory to all other applicants because an individual's ethnicity does not affect loss potential.

Direct Your Learning

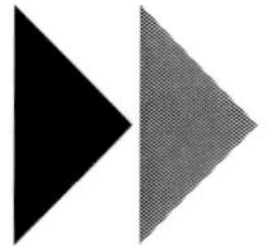

3

Personal Auto Insurance: Liability, Medical Payments, and UM

Educational Objectives

After learning the content of this assignment, you should be able to:

1. Summarize the sections of the Personal Auto Policy.
2. Explain how the words and phrases included in the Definitions section of the Personal Auto Policy are used to determine whether coverage applies and, if so, whether it is modified, excluded, or limited.
3. Summarize each of the provisions in Part A—Liability Coverage of the Personal Auto Policy.
4. Summarize each of the provisions in Part B—Medical Payments Coverage of the Personal Auto Policy.
5. Summarize each of the provisions in Part C—Uninsured Motorists Coverage of the Personal Auto Policy.
6. Describe underinsured motorists insurance in terms of:
   - Its purpose
   - The ways in which it can vary by state
7. Given a case describing a claim involving an individual or a family with a Personal Auto Policy (PAP) that includes liability, medical payments, and uninsured motorists coverage, determine what is covered, excluded, or limited, and for what amounts.

Outline

- **Overview of the Personal Auto Policy**
  - A. Declarations
  - B. Agreement and Definitions
  - C. Overview of Coverages
  - D. Endorsements
- **Personal Auto Policy Definitions**
  - A. Purpose of PAP Definitions
  - B. Important PAP Definitions
- **Part A—Liability Coverage**
  - A. Insuring Agreement
    1. Damages and Defense Costs Covered
    2. Persons and Organizations Insured
  - B. Supplementary Payments
  - C. Exclusions
    1. Intentional Injury
    2. Property Owned or Transported
    3. Property Rented to, Used by, or in the Care of the Insured
    4. Bodily Injury to an Employee of an Insured
    5. Public or Livery Conveyance
    6. Garage Business Use
    7. Other Business Use
    8. Vehicle Used Without Reasonable Belief of Being Entitled
    9. Nuclear Energy Liability Losses
    10. Vehicles With Fewer Than Four Wheels or Designed for Off-Road Use
    11. Other Vehicles Owned by Insured or Available for Insured's Regular Use
    12. Vehicles Owned by or Available for Family Member's Regular Use
    13. Racing
  - D. Limit of Liability
  - E. Out of State Coverage
  - F. Financial Responsibility
  - G. Other Insurance
- **Part B—Medical Payments Coverage**
  - A. Insuring Agreement
  - B. Exclusions
    1. Motorized Vehicles With Fewer Than Four Wheels
    2. Public or Livery Conveyance
    3. Vehicles Used as a Residence or Premises
    4. Injury During the Course of Employment
    5. Other Vehicles Owned by Insured or Available for Insured's Regular Use
    6. Vehicles Owned by or Available for Family Member's Regular Use
    7. Vehicle Occupied Without Reasonable Belief of Being Entitled
    8. Vehicles Used in the Business of an Insured
    9. Bodily Injury From Nuclear Weapons or War
    10. Nuclear Radiation
    11. Racing
  - C. Limit of Liability
  - D. Other Insurance
- **Part C—Uninsured Motorists Coverage**
  - A. Insuring Agreement
    1. Insured Persons
    2. Uninsured Motor Vehicles
  - B. Exclusions
    1. Owned But Not Insured Vehicle
    2. Owned Vehicle With Primary UM Coverage in Other Policy
    3. Claim Settlement That Prejudices Insurer's Right of Recovery
    4. Public or Livery Conveyance
    5. Vehicle Used Without Reasonable Belief of Being Entitled
    6. No Benefit to Workers Compensation or Disability Benefits Insurer
    7. Punitive Damages
  - C. Limit of Liability
  - D. Other Insurance
  - E. Arbitration
- **UM/UIM Endorsements and State Variations**
  - A. Purpose of Coverage

s.m.a.r.t.® tips

Actively capture information by using the open space in the SMART Review Notes to write out key concepts. Putting information into your own words is an effective way to push that information into your memory.

Outline

For each assignment, you should define or describe each of the Key Words and Phrases and answer each of the Review and Application Questions.

Educational Objective 1

Summarize the sections of the Personal Auto Policy.

Review Questions

1-1. List the information found on the Declarations page of an Insurance Services Office, Inc. (ISO) Personal Auto Policy (PAP).

1-2. Identify the information contained in the Agreement and Definitions page of the PAP.

1-3. Contrast the coverage provided under Part A of the PAP with the coverage provided under Part D.

Application Question

1-4. At the renewal of his policy, George switched insurers for the PAP covering his family's vehicles. Explain how George can use the Declarations page to compare the new policy with the policy from the previous insurer.

Educational Objective 2

Explain how the words and phrases included in the Definitions section of the Personal Auto Policy are used to determine whether coverage applies and, if so, whether it is modified, excluded, or limited.

Review Questions

2-1. What are two purposes of the Personal Auto Policy (PAP) Definitions?

2-2. When is an unnamed spouse of the named insured considered "you" and "your" according to the PAP Definitions?

Educational Objective 3

Summarize each of the provisions in Part A—Liability Coverage of the Personal Auto Policy.

Key Words and Phrases

Compensatory damages

Split-limits basis

Single-limits basis

Prejudgment interest

Supplementary payments

Attachment

Postjudgment interest

Public or livery conveyance

Review Questions

3-1. Explain what occurs if the cost to defend an insured under the Personal Auto Policy (PAP) exceeds the policy limit of liability.

3-2. Describe the situation in which an insurer would pay the cost of a bail bond for an insured under a PAP.

3-3. Explain the intent behind the PAP exclusion that eliminates liability coverage for an insured while employed or engaged in the business of selling, repairing, servicing, storing, or parking vehicles designed for use mainly on public highways.

Application Question

3-4. Sara works as a maid for Charlie. Charlie insures his auto under a PAP. He asks Sara to accompany him to the grocery store. While en route, he drives the car into a pole, causing bodily injury to Sara. Workers compensation benefits are not required for domestic employees in the state where the accident occurred. Explain what liability coverage Charlie has for Sara's claims against him.

Educational Objective 4

Summarize each of the provisions in Part B—Medical Payments Coverage of the Personal Auto Policy.

Review Questions

4-1. Describe the two classes of insureds covered by Part B of the Personal Auto Policy (PAP).

4-2. Describe the exception to the PAP Part B exclusion that eliminates coverage for injuries sustained by an insured while occupying a vehicle (other than a covered auto) that is owned by or available for the regular use of a family member.

4-3. Explain how a coverage issue is resolved in a claim from a driver who has Part B coverage under a PAP and who was injured while driving a borrowed vehicle whose owner also has Part B coverage under a PAP.

Application Question

4-4. Elizabeth's son, Sam, is a family member as defined in his mother's PAP. Although Sam is old enough to drive, after having been involved in several serious accidents, he has promised his mother that he will not drive. However, late one Saturday night, Sam becomes bored and decides to go for a drive. He takes his mother's car while she is sleeping. While driving, he strikes a parked car and is injured. Explain what medical expense coverage Sam may have under Elizabeth's PAP.

Educational Objective 5

Summarize each of the provisions in Part C—Uninsured Motorists Coverage of the Personal Auto Policy.

Key Words and Phrases

Uninsured motor vehicle

Arbitration

Review Questions

5-1. Describe the four categories of criteria a vehicle must meet to be covered by Part C of the Personal Auto Policy (PAP).

5-2. Explain the purpose of the PAP Part C exclusion that eliminates uninsured motorists (UM) coverage for a claim that the insured settles without the insurer's consent if such a settlement prejudices the insurer's right to recover payment.

5-3. Describe the Part C policy provision that is intended to prevent "stacking" of UM payments under a policy that covers more than one car owned by the named insured.

5-4. Explain whether a decision resulting from arbitration, the dispute resolution method designated by Part C of the PAP, is binding upon both parties when the amount of damages agreed on exceeds the minimum limit for bodily injury specified by the state's financial responsibility law.

Application Question

5-5. Doug is employed as a delivery driver for a pizza restaurant. When delivering pizza, he uses his own vehicle, which is insured under his PAP. Doug is seriously injured during a pizza delivery when his car is struck from behind by a hit-and-run driver. The pizza restaurant's workers compensation insurer, Delmond Insurance, pays Doug for his medical expenses and lost wages. Delmond Insurance decides to seek reimbursement from Doug's PAP insurer under Part C of Doug's policy. Explain the basis of Delmond's claim and what will likely occur in Delmond's attempt to assert it.

Educational Objective 6

Describe underinsured motorists insurance in terms of:

- **Its purpose**
- **The ways in which it can vary by state**

Review Questions

6-1. Describe the conditions in which underinsured motorists (UIM) coverage applies.

6-2. Aside from using ISO's Underinsured Motorists Coverage Endorsement (PP 03 11), explain how states can provide UIM coverage as a supplement to the UM coverage in the Personal Auto Policy (PAP).

6-3. Describe the key criterion that determines when a UIM endorsement with a limits trigger applies.

Application Question

6-4. Carol and Richard each live in a state that applies a damages trigger to a UIM endorsement. Carol has an auto liability policy with a $75,000 UIM limit. Richard purchased auto liability coverage with a $125,000 single limit. Richard causes an auto accident in which Carol is injured.

a. Explain how Carol's UIM coverage will be affected if her damages amount to $200,000.

b. Explain how Carol's UIM coverage will be affected if her damages amount to $100,000.

Educational Objective 7

Given a case describing a claim involving an individual or a family with a Personal Auto Policy (PAP) that includes liability, medical payments, and uninsured motorists coverage, determine what is covered, excluded, or limited, and for what amounts.

Application Question

7-1. Barbara was driving her vehicle, and her friend Kevin was a passenger. They were starting a one-week visit with Kevin's parents, who live in the same state about 150 miles south of the town where Barbara and Kevin live.

Barbara's vehicle is insured under a PAP listing her as the named insured. These are the coverages included in the policy:

Coverage A—Liability: $50,000 Each person

$100,000 Each occurrence

Property Damage: $50,000

Coverage B—Medical Payments: $1,000 Each person

Coverage C—Uninsured Motorists: $50,000 Each person

$100,000 Each occurrence

To lower her premiums, Barbara decided not to carry Coverage D—Damage to Your Auto on her five-year old vehicle.

About one hour into the trip, as they were traveling in the southbound lanes of the highway, a northbound vehicle crossed the median and struck Barbara's vehicle. This four-door sedan was operated by Louise, who died at the scene. As part of the accident investigation, it was determined that Louise suffered a heart attack, which caused her to lose control of her vehicle and cross the highway.

Louise had a PAP listing herself and her husband as named insureds. These are the coverages included in the policy:

Coverage A—Liability: $250,000 Each person

$500,000 Each occurrence

Property Damage: $100,000.

Coverage B—Medical Payments: $5,000 Each person

Coverage C—Uninsured Motorists: $100,000 Each person

$300,000 Each occurrence

a. Barbara was severely injured as a result of the accident, for which the court finds Louise liable. Damages are $210,000 for Barbara's hospital and rehabilitation expenses as well as lost wages for six months. Which policy will cover these expenses and for what amount?

b. In addition to the damages for medical expenses and lost wages, the court awards $50,000 in prejudgment interest to Barbara. Explain whether this amount is covered under the PAP, which policy would respond, and for what amount.

c. Barbara's vehicle was carrying several boxes of Kevin's household property, which he intended to store at his parents' home. Is damage to this property as the result of the accident covered under Barbara's PAP?

Answers to Assignment 3 Questions

NOTE: These answers are provided to give students a basic understanding of acceptable types of responses. They often are not the only valid answers and are not intended to provide an exhaustive response to the questions.

Educational Objective 1

1-1. The Declarations page of the PAP can include the name and mailing address of both the insurer and the named insured; the policy period; and the name and address of the producer, if applicable. It also may include a description of the covered autos, limits of liability, premium and rating information, and any endorsements added to the policy.

1-2. The Agreement and Definitions page of the PAP includes a general agreement stating that the insurer is providing the coverage subject to payment of premium and to the terms of the policy. Definitions are also provided for words and phrases used throughout the policy.

1-3. Part A provides liability coverage and protects the insurer against claims for bodily injury or property damage arising out of the operation of an auto. Part D of the PAP covers physical damage to a covered auto and includes collision and other than collision coverages.

1-4. When comparing the two policies, George can look at the Declarations page of each policy to review the dates of coverage, the descriptions of covered autos, limits of liability, endorsement listings, and premiums in order to determine whether any changes have been made and whether the information is accurate.

Educational Objective 2

2-1. The PAP Definitions section is written in simple language designed to be easily understood by individuals who may not be familiar with insurance terminology. The definitions clarify to whom, to what, when, and under what circumstances coverage, exclusions, insuring agreements, and other policy provisions apply; these definitions are crucial to understanding the policy provisions.

2-2. An unnamed spouse of the named insured is considered "you" (and "your") provided that he or she is a resident of the same household. However, when the spouse moves out of the household and remains married to the insured, then the spouse is considered "you" for another ninety days or until the policy expires—whichever comes first, and ceases if the spouse is named on another policy.

Educational Objective 3

3-1. The insurer agrees to defend the insured and pay all legal costs the insured may incur in a liability suit—even if the combined costs exceed the limit of liability. In other words, the insurer is obligated to pay defense costs in addition to the policy limits.

3-2. The cost of a bail bond is covered under the PAP's Supplementary Payments provision. The insurer agrees to pay up to $250 for the cost of a bail bond (bail bond premium) required because of an accident that results in bodily injury or property damage covered by the policy.

3-3. The intent behind this PAP exclusion is to exclude a loss exposure that should be covered by a commercial auto policy, such as a garage policy purchased by the owner of the business.

3-4. The PAP excludes liability coverage for bodily injury to an employee of an insured who is injured during the course of employment. Sara is employed by Charlie, the insured, and was injured during the course of her employment. However, an exception to this exclusion is injury to a domestic employee in the course of employment when workers compensation benefits are not required. Therefore, despite the exclusion, Charlie's PAP should provide coverage for Sara's liability claim against him.

Educational Objective 4

4-1. Part B covers two classes of insureds:

- The named insured and "family members" (as defined in the PAP) are covered for their medical expenses if they are injured while occupying a motor vehicle or as pedestrians when struck by a motor vehicle designed for use mainly on public roads.
- Any other person while occupying a covered auto.

4-2. The exclusion does not apply to the named insured and spouse occupying such a vehicle.

4-3. For the driver of a nonowned vehicle, the driver's own PAP is excess over any other collectible auto insurance that pays medical or funeral expenses, including the PAP of the owner of the vehicle.

4-4. Part B of the PAP contains an exclusion that eliminates coverage if an insured sustains an injury while using a vehicle without a reasonable belief that he is entitled to do so. Taking his mother's car while she was sleeping and having made a previous promise that he would not drive would appear to place Sam within the application of this exclusion and preclude coverage for his injuries in this accident. However, the medical payments exclusion does not apply to a family member who uses an owned auto of the named insured. For insurance purposes, it is assumed that a family member has permission to use another family member's car. Therefore, Sam's medical expenses should be covered by his mother's PAP within the limits of her policy.

Educational Objective 5

5-1. To be covered by Part C, a vehicle must be a land vehicle or trailer that meets any of these criteria:

- No bodily injury liability insurance or bond applies to the vehicle at the time of the accident.
- A bodily injury liability policy or bond is in force, but the limit for bodily injury is less than the minimum amount required by the state's financial responsibility law.
- The vehicle is a hit-and-run vehicle whose owner or operator cannot be identified.
- A bodily injury policy or bond applies at the time of the accident, but the insurance or bonding company (a) denies coverage or (b) is or becomes insolvent.

5-2. The purpose of this exclusion is to protect the insurer's right to assert a subrogation action against the party who is legally responsible for the insured's injuries.

5-3. The terms in the limit of liability provision are intended to prevent stacking. The terms state that the limits shown in the declarations are the most that will be paid regardless of the number of insured persons, claims made, vehicles or premiums shown in the declarations, or vehicles involved in the accident.

5-4. If the amount agreed on in arbitration exceeds the statutory limit, either party can demand the right to a trial within sixty days of the arbitrators' decision. Otherwise, the arbitrators' decision is binding.

5-5. In some states, if an injured employee receives workers compensation benefits, the workers compensation insurer has a legal right to recover the amount of the benefits from a negligent third party through subrogation. If an employee receives workers compensation benefits for an injury involving an uninsured, at-fault driver, the workers compensation insurer could sue the driver or attempt to make a claim under the injured employee's UM coverage, which is what Delmond Insurance is attempting to do. However, Part C of the PAP contains an exclusion that prevents any insurer from benefiting directly or indirectly under a workers compensation law. That exclusion will likely prevent Delmond from obtaining reimbursement under Doug's PAP UM coverage.

Educational Objective 6

6-1. Underinsured motorists (UIM) coverage applies when a negligent driver is insured for at least the minimum required financial responsibility limits but the policy's liability limits are insufficient to pay the insured's damages.

6-2. Aside from using ISO's Underinsured Motorists Coverage Endorsement (PP 03 11), states can provide coverage as a supplement to the UM coverage in the PAP by using either a state-specific UIM endorsement or a single, state-specific endorsement providing both UM and UIM coverages that replaces the UM coverage of the standard PAP.

6-3. The key criterion for UIM protection with a limits trigger is that the liability limits of the other party's policy are less than the insured's UIM limits.

6-4. These answers address questions regarding Carol's UIM coverage:

a. If Carol's damages amount to $200,000, her UIM coverage will be triggered because Richard's policy limit is less than Carol's damages.

b. If Carol's damages amount to $100,000, her UIM coverage will not be triggered because her damages are less than Richard's limit.

Educational Objective 7

7-1. These answers apply to questions about Barbara and Kevin's insurance claims:

a. Because Louise was found liable for the accident, her PAP will cover this loss. The claim representative confirms that the vehicle Louise was operating is a covered vehicle on the policy and that Louise is listed as an insured. The $210,000 in damages is within the $250,000 each person liability limit shown on the policy, so the damages will be paid in full.

b. Prejudgment interest is covered under the PAP and allows Barbara to receive interest on a judgment from the time the accident occurred or a lawsuit was filed to the time the judgment was handed down by the court. Because Louise was found legally liable for this accident, the prejudgment interest will be paid as part of the award for damages under Part A of her PAP. This payment is, however, subject to the bodily injury limit of liability. Because damages in the amount of $210,000 have already been paid and the each person limit on Louise's PAP is $250,000, only $40,000 is available to pay the prejudgment interest amount.

c. Damage to this property is not covered. The PAP includes an exclusion for property damage to property owned or being transported by the insured. The "property rented to, used by, or in the care of the insured" exclusion would also apply. Barbara's liability for any damage to Kevin's property is not covered under the PAP.

Direct Your Learning

4

Personal Auto Insurance: Physical Damage and Endorsements

Educational Objectives

After learning the content of this assignment, you should be able to:

1. Summarize each of the provisions in Part D—Coverage for Damage to Your Auto of the Personal Auto Policy.
2. Given a case describing an auto physical damage claim, determine whether Part D—Coverage for Damage to Your Auto of the Personal Auto Policy would cover the claim and, if so, the amount the insurer would pay for the claim.
3. Describe the insured's duties following a covered auto accident or loss as shown in Part E of the Personal Auto Policy.
4. Summarize each of the general provisions in Part F of the Personal Auto Policy.
5. Describe the Personal Auto Policy endorsements that are used to handle common auto loss exposures.
6. Given a case describing a claim involving an individual or a family with a Personal Auto Policy, determine what is covered, excluded, or limited, and for what amounts.

Outline

- **Part D—Coverage for Damage to Your Auto**
  - A. Insuring Agreement
    - 1. Collision Coverage
    - 2. Other Than Collision Coverage
    - 3. Nonowned Autos
    - 4. Deductibles
  - B. Transportation Expenses
  - C. Exclusions
    - 1. Public or Livery Conveyance
    - 2. Wear and Tear, Freezing, Breakdown, and Road Damage to Tires
    - 3. Radioactive Contamination or War
    - 4. Electronic Equipment
    - 5. Media and Accessories
    - 6. Government Destruction or Confiscation
    - 7. Trailer, Camper Body, or Motor Home
    - 8. Nonowned Auto Used Without Reasonable Belief of Being Entitled
    - 9. Radar and Laser Detection Equipment
    - 10. Customizing Equipment
    - 11. Nonowned Auto Used in Garage Business
    - 12. Racing
    - 13. Rental Vehicles
  - D. Limit of Liability
  - E. Payment of Loss
  - F. No Benefit to Bailee
  - G. Other Sources of Recovery
  - H. Appraisal
- **Part D—Coverage for Damage to Your Auto Case Study**
  - A. Case Facts
  - B. Case Analysis Tools
  - C. Determination of Coverage
  - D. Determination of Amounts Payable
- **Part E—Duties After an Accident or Loss**
  - A. General Duties
  - B. Additional Duties for Uninsured Motorists Coverage
  - C. Additional Duties for Physical Damage Coverage
- **Part F—General Provisions**
  - A. Bankruptcy of Insured
  - B. Changes in the Policy
  - C. Fraud
  - D. Legal Action Against the Insurer
  - E. Insurer's Right to Recover Payment
  - F. Policy Period and Territory
  - G. Termination
    - 1. Cancellation
    - 2. Nonrenewal
    - 3. Automatic Termination
    - 4. Other Termination Provisions
  - H. Transfer of Insured's Interest in the Policy
  - I. Two or More Auto Policies
- **Common Endorsements to the Personal Auto Policy**
  - A. Miscellaneous Type Vehicle Endorsement
  - B. Snowmobile Endorsement
  - C. Trailer/Camper Body Coverage (Maximum Limit of Liability)
  - D. Extended Non-Owned Coverage—Vehicles Furnished or Available for Regular Use
  - E. Named Non-Owner Coverage
  - F. Auto Loan/Lease Coverage
  - G. Limited Mexico Coverage
  - H. Excess Electronic Equipment Coverage
  - I. Coverage for Damage to Your Auto (Maximum Limit of Liability)
  - J. Optional Limits Transportation Expenses Coverage
  - K. Towing and Labor Costs Coverage
- **Personal Auto Policy Coverage Case Study**
  - A. Case Facts
  - B. Case Analysis Tools
  - C. Determination of Coverage
  - D. Determination of Amounts Payable

s.m.a.r.t.® tips The SMART Online Practice Exams can be tailored to cover specific assignments, so you can focus your studies on topics you want to master.

For each assignment, you should define or describe each of the Key Words and Phrases and answer each of the Review and Application Questions.

Educational Objective 1

Summarize each of the provisions in Part D—Coverage for Damage to Your Auto of the Personal Auto Policy.

Key Words and Phrases

Physical damage coverages

Deductible

Other than collision (OTC) coverage

Transportation expenses

Actual cash value (ACV)

Appraisal

Review Questions

1-1. Explain John's options for collecting damages if he has collision coverage for his car and another driver causes an accident that damages John's car.

1-2. Explain how often an insured can drive a rented or borrowed auto and expect his or her auto physical damage insurance to cover the vehicle.

1-3. List three reasons for deductibles in auto physical damage coverage.

1-4. Explain whether, if an insured decides to race his sports car against the driver of another car on a city street, damage to his car resulting from a collision that occurs during this activity would be excluded under his PAP collision coverage.

Application Question

1-5. Jack rents a car from XYZ Rental Car Agency. He declines the damage waiver offered by XYZ at a substantial extra cost. While driving the rental car, Jack is involved in an auto accident with another car. Who is at fault is being contested, but, in the meantime, the rental car is not available to be rented while it is being repaired. XYZ has demanded reimbursement from Jack for its loss of the income the car would have earned in rental fees of $40 per day. Will Jack's PAP collision coverage for his covered auto help him in this situation and, if so, to what extent?

Educational Objective 2

Given a case describing an auto physical damage claim, determine whether Part D—Coverage for Damage to Your Auto of the Personal Auto Policy would cover the claim and, if so, the amount the insurer would pay for the claim.

Application Questions

2-1. Lucia has a PAP with coverage for other than collision (OTC) loss that is subject to a $200 deductible. However, she did not purchase collision coverage and is not insured for those losses. What dollar amount, if any, will Lucia's insurer pay under her PAP for each of these losses? If a loss is not covered or not fully covered, explain why. Treat each loss separately.

a. Lucia parks her car at the grocery store and goes shopping. She returns just in time to see another vehicle strike her car and then quickly leave. Assume that the state where Lucia's car is principally garaged does not allow uninsured motorists property damage coverage. Her mechanic estimates that the repairs will cost $1,000.

b. Lucia's factory-installed car radio valued at $400 was stolen from her car.

2-2. Tony has a PAP with coverage for OTC loss that is subject to a $500 deductible. After enjoying a night out at the movies with his friends, Tony discovers that his car has been stolen from the theatre parking lot. He immediately reports the loss to the police and to his insurer. The next morning, Tony rents a substitute auto for $40 a day. Thirty-six hours after the theft, the police report that they have found the car intact. Tony determines that the only items stolen were his compact discs (CDs), valued at approximately $500.

a. What dollar amount, if any, will Tony's PAP pay for his rented auto?

b. What dollar amount, if any, will Tony's PAP pay for the rented auto if his car was recovered after having been missing for a total of seven days?

Educational Objective 3

Describe the insured's duties following a covered auto accident or loss as shown in Part E of the Personal Auto Policy.

Key Word or Phrase

Proof of loss

Review Questions

3-1. List the seven general duties a person seeking coverage under the PAP must perform after an accident or a loss.

3-2. Describe the details a person seeking coverage under the PAP should include when notifying the insurer that an accident or a loss has occurred.

3-3. Describe two additional duties required if the insured is seeking payment under Coverage C—Uninsured Motorists Coverage of the PAP.

3-4. Part E of a PAP states the general duties that the insured must perform after an accident or a loss. Additional duties are required if the insured is seeking payment under Part D—Coverage for Damage to Your Auto.

a. Explain why it is important for insureds to perform the duties after a loss as outlined in Part E of the PAP.

b. Describe the three additional duties required if the insured is seeking payment under Part D of the PAP.

Educational Objective 4

Summarize each of the general provisions in Part F of the Personal Auto Policy.

Key Words and Phrases

Liberalization Clause

Policy termination

Cancellation

Review Questions

4-1. Briefly describe each of the general provisions in Part F of the PAP:

a. Bankruptcy of the Insured

b. Policy Period and Territory

c. Two or More Policies

4-2. Identify four changes an insured can make during the policy period that can result in a premium increase or decrease.

4-3. Describe the obligations that an insured must fulfill before he or she can sue the insurer.

4-4. List the three reasons for which an insurer can cancel a policy that has been in force for sixty or more days.

Application Question

4-5. Explain how the PAP would respond in the following situations based on the provisions contained in Part F of the policy.

a. The insured deliberately burns his car and submits a claim under the policy's physical damage coverage.

b. Henry has replaced his current auto insurance policy with a new insurer. What must he do to cancel his original auto policy, which was issued by a different insurer?

Educational Objective 5

Describe the Personal Auto Policy endorsements that are used to handle common auto loss exposures.

Review Questions

5-1. Explain why an insured may want to include an optional passenger exclusion to a Miscellaneous Type Vehicle endorsement.

5-2. Explain why an insured would purchase an Extended Non-Owned Coverage—Vehicles Furnished or Available for Regular Use endorsement.

5-3. Describe how a stated amount of insurance may not provide coverage for that amount when a Coverage for Damage to Your Auto endorsement has been added to the PAP.

Educational Objective 6

Given a case describing a claim involving an individual or a family with a Personal Auto Policy, determine what is covered, excluded, or limited, and for what amounts.

Application Question

6-1. Mark was driving through a local park when he became distracted and struck a parked vehicle. Mark's vehicle sustained $4,200 in damage. The parked vehicle, owned by Nathan, sustained $5,000 in damage and was pushed into another parked vehicle, resulting in $2,100 in damage to that vehicle. Two occupants of the first parked vehicle were seriously injured. One of these occupants, Nathan, incurred $24,000 in medical expenses. The other occupant, Denise, incurred $6,700 in medical expenses. Mark was held responsible for the accident. The state where Mark lives does not have a no-fault insurance law.

Mark has a Personal Auto Policy (PAP) with these coverages and limits:

Part A—Liability Coverage: $100,000 per person/$300,000 per accident

Property Damage: $25,000.

Part B—Medical Payments: $5,000 per person

Part D—Damage to Your Auto: $500 deductible – OTC

$1,000 deductible – Collision

a. How would Mark's policy respond for the injuries and damage to Nathan's vehicle?

b. How would Mark's policy respond for the damages to the second parked vehicle?

c. How would Mark's policy respond for the damage to his vehicle in this accident?

Answers to Assignment 4 Questions

NOTE: These answers are provided to give students a basic understanding of acceptable types of responses. They often are not the only valid answers and are not intended to provide an exhaustive response to the questions.

Educational Objective 1

1-1. John can collect either from the other driver (or the driver's insurer) or from his own insurer. If John collects from his insurer, that insurer has the right to recover payment from the driver (or the driver's insurer). This recovery is referred to as subrogation.

1-2. The vehicle would be covered if driven occasionally by the insured. However, if the insured regularly drives the rented or borrowed vehicle, or if it is made available for the insured's regular use, the insured's coverage will not apply.

1-3. Insurers require deductibles in auto physical damage coverage for several reasons:

- To reduce small claims
- To hold down premiums
- To encourage insureds to be careful in protecting their cars against damage or theft

1-4. The damage to the insured's car from racing would probably not be excluded. Loss to a covered auto is excluded if the auto is damaged while located in a facility designed for racing if the auto is being used to prepare for, practice for, or compete in any prearranged racing or speed contest. It appears that this race was not prearranged.

1-5. Part D of Jack's PAP provides coverage for transportation expenses. Under this provision, the rental car is covered as a nonowned auto, and the rental company's lost income while the car is being repaired is covered. However, the transportation expenses are limited to a maximum of $20 per day and $600 for each covered loss. Also, although transportation expenses do not have a dollar-amount deductible, they are subject to a twenty-four-hour waiting period. Therefore, Jack's insurer would pay only $20 a day for XYZ's lost income, and the first day's loss would not be paid. Jack should also be aware that, at $20 per day and a maximum of $600, he has only thirty days of coverage ($600 divided by $20).

Educational Objective 2

2-1. These answers address questions about Luica's PAP:

a. In order for Lucia's PAP to cover these repairs, she would need collision coverage. Because Lucia has only other than collision coverage, her insurer will not cover the expense to repair her auto.

b. Because Lucia's radio was factory-installed, it is covered (less the deductible). So her insurer will pay $200 ($400 minus $200) for the loss.

2-2. These answers address questions about Tony's PAP:

a. Tony's PAP imposes a two-day waiting period before transportation expense reimbursement begins. Because his car was recovered thirty-six hours after the theft, Tony's insurer will not cover the expense for the rental car.

b. Although the cost of renting a temporary substitute auto is insured under the Transportation Expenses coverage of Tony's PAP, that coverage is limited to $20 a day, not to exceed a maximum of $600. (The deductible does not apply to the Transportation Expense coverage.) The car was missing for a total of seven days. However, since the claim involves a total theft of the car, there is a two-day waiting period. Therefore, Tony will receive reimbursement of $100—$20 per day for his transportation expenses for five days—to offset the $280 he paid for the rental car.

Educational Objective 3

3-1. A person seeking coverage under the PAP must perform seven duties:

- Provide prompt notification of the details of the accident or loss to the insurer
- Cooperate with the insurer in the investigation, settlement, or defense of any claim or suit
- Submit copies of notices or legal papers in connection with the accident or loss to the insurer
- Agree to submit to a physical examination if requested by the insurer
- Agree to be examined under oath if required by the insurer
- Authorize the insurer to obtain medical reports and other pertinent records
- Submit a proof of loss when required by the insurer

3-2. The notification should include details such as how, when, and where the accident happened, as well as the names and addresses of any injured persons and witnesses.

3-3. A person seeking benefits under Uninsured Motorists Coverage must perform two additional duties:

- Promptly notify the police if a hit-and-run driver is involved
- Send a copy of the legal papers to the insurance company if the person seeking coverage sues the uninsured motorist

3-4. These answers address questions regarding Parts D and E of a PAP:

a. It is important for insureds to perform the duties after a loss as outlined in Part E because if the insured does not perform them and this failure is prejudicial to the insurer, the insurer has no obligation to provide coverage and to pay for the loss.

b. There are three additional duties required if the insured is seeking payment under Part D of the PAP:

- The person seeking coverage must take reasonable steps after a loss to protect a covered auto or nonowned auto and its equipment from further loss.
- If a covered auto or nonowned auto is stolen, the person seeking coverage must promptly notify the police of the theft.
- The person seeking coverage must permit the insurer to inspect and appraise the damaged property before its repair or disposal.

Educational Objective 4

4-1. These answers address questions regarding the general provisions in Part F of the PAP:

a. This provision states that if the insured declares bankruptcy or becomes insolvent, the insurer is not relieved of any obligations under the policy.

b. According to this provision, coverage applies only to accidents and losses that occur during the policy period shown on the declarations page. The policy territory includes the United States, U.S. territories and possessions, Puerto Rico, and Canada. The policy also applies to a covered auto while being transported among ports of the U.S., Puerto Rico, or Canada. Coverage does not apply anywhere outside the policy territory.

c. According to this provision, if two or more auto policies issued to the named insured by the same insurer apply to the same accident, the insurer's maximum limit of liability is the highest applicable limit of liability under any one policy.

4-2. Changes an insured can make during the policy period that can result in a premium increase or decrease include changes in:

- The number, type, or use of insured vehicles
- The operators using insured vehicles
- The place of principal garaging of insured vehicles
- The coverage provided, deductibles, or limits of liability

4-3. No legal action can be brought against the insurer until the insured has fully complied with all of the policy terms. In addition, under Part A—Liability Coverage, no legal action can be brought against the insurer unless the insurer agrees in writing that the insured has an obligation to pay damages or the amount of the insurer's obligation has been finally determined by a judgment after a trial.

4-4. These are three reasons for which an insurer can cancel a policy that has been in force for sixty or more days:

- The premium has not been paid.
- The driver's license of an insured has been suspended or revoked during the policy period (or since the last annual anniversary of the original effective date if the policy is for other than one year).
- The policy has been obtained by a material misrepresentation.

4-5. These answers address questions regarding how the PAP would respond based on provisions contained in Part F of the policy:

a. Because the PAP contains a fraud provision stating that no coverage exists for any insured who makes fraudulent statements or engages in fraudulent conduct in connection with any accident or loss for which a claim is made, the insurer would not be obligated to pay this claim.

b. To comply with the cancellation provision, Henry can cancel the original policy anytime during the policy period by returning the policy to the insurer or by giving advance written notice of the date the cancellation is to become effective.

Educational Objective 5

5-1. A motorcycle owner who never carries passengers can elect this exclusion in exchange for a lower premium.

5-2. The unendorsed Personal Auto Policy (PAP) excludes liability and medical payments coverage for vehicles furnished or made available for the regular use of the named insured and family members. This exclusion can be eliminated by adding the Extended Non-Owned Coverage—Vehicles Furnished or Available for Regular Use (PP 03 06 01 05) endorsement to the PAP. The endorsement provides liability coverage for any vehicle furnished or available for the regular use of the named individual and for family members who are indicated in the schedule. For example, if Alice is furnished with a company car by her employer, this endorsement would provide liability and/or medical payments coverage on an excess basis.

5-3. Even though the endorsement indicates a stated amount of insurance, it may not provide coverage for that amount in the event of a total loss to the vehicle. Rather, the insurer's maximum limit of liability for a covered loss is limited to the lowest of three values: the stated amount shown in the schedule or in the declarations; the actual cash value of the stolen or damaged property; or the amount necessary to repair or replace the property with other property of like kind and quality.

If, for example, the stated amount of insurance is less than the vehicle's actual cash value or the amount necessary to repair or replace the property, the stated amount is used as the basis of the loss settlement. However, if the stated amount of insurance is greater than the vehicle's actual cash value or the amount necessary to repair or replace the property, the lower amount is the basis for payment. In any case, the amount paid is reduced by any applicable deductible shown in the endorsement schedule or policy declarations.

Educational Objective 6

6-1. These answers address questions about Mark's accident:

a. Because Mark was found responsible for the accident, his insurer would pay a total of $35,700, which is within the limits of his policy. This amount includes these payments:

- Coverage A—Bodily Injury: $24,000 in medical expenses for Nathan
- Coverage A—Bodily Injury: $ 6,700 in medical expenses for Denise
- Coverage A—Property Damage: $5,000 in damage to Nathan's vehicle

b. Mark's insurer would pay $2,100 for this damage under Coverage A—Property Damage.

c. Mark's insurer would pay $3,200 under Coverage D—Damage to Your Auto—Collision ($4,200 total damage minus $1,000 deductible).

Direct Your Learning

5

Homeowners Section I

Educational Objectives

After learning the content of this assignment, you should be able to:

1. Describe how individuals and families can use the Insurance Services Office, Inc., (ISO) 2011 Homeowners insurance program to address their personal risk management needs.
2. Describe the Homeowners 3—Special Form (HO-3) in terms of:
   - Its structure and the coverages it provides
   - The role of endorsements in modifying it
   - The factors considered in rating it
3. Describe what is insured by each of these coverages contained in the 2011 Homeowners 3—Special Form (HO-3) policy:
   - Coverage A—Dwelling
   - Coverage B—Other Structures
   - Coverage C—Personal Property
   - Coverage D—Loss of Use
   - Additional Coverages
4. Describe what is covered and what is excluded by these provisions in the 2011 Homeowners 3—Special Form (HO-3) policy:
   - Perils Insured Against for Coverages A and B
   - Perils Insured Against for Coverage C
   - Section I—Exclusions
5. Summarize each of the 2011 Homeowners 3—Special Form (HO-3) policy provisions in Section I—Conditions.

5

Educational Objectives, continued

6. Given a scenario describing a homeowners property claim, determine whether the 2011 HO-3 policy Section I—Property Coverages would cover the claim and, if so, the amount the insurer would pay for the claim.

Outline

- **ISO Homeowners Coverage**
- **Overview of Homeowners Form HO-3**
  - A. Structure of Homeowners Form HO-3
    1. Declarations
    2. Agreement and Definitions
    3. Section I—Property Coverages
    4. Section II—Liability Coverages
  - B. Role of Endorsements
  - C. Factors Considered in Rating
- **HO-3 Section I—Property Coverages**
  - A. Coverage A—Dwelling
  - B. Coverage B—Other Structures
  - C. Coverage C—Personal Property
    1. Special Limits of Liability
    2. Property Not Covered
  - D. Coverage D—Loss of Use
  - E. Additional Coverages
- **HO-3 Section I—Perils Insured Against and Exclusions**
  - A. Perils Insured Against for Coverages A and B
  - B. Perils Insured Against for Coverage C
  - C. Section I—Exclusions
- **HO-3 Section I—Conditions**
  - A. Insurable Interest and Limit of Liability
  - B. Deductible
  - C. Your Duties After Loss
  - D. Loss Settlement
  - E. Loss to a Pair or Set
  - F. Appraisal
  - G. Other Insurance and Service Agreement
  - H. Our Option
  - I. Loss Payment
  - J. Abandonment of Property
  - K. Mortgage Clause
  - L. No Benefit to Bailee
  - M. Loss Payable Clause
- **2011 HO-3 Section I—Property Coverage Case Study**
  - A. Case Facts
  - B. Necessary Reference Materials
  - C. Overview of Steps
  - D. Determination of Coverage
    1. DICE Analysis Step 1: Declarations
    2. DICE Analysis Step 2: Insuring Agreement
    3. DICE Analysis Step 3: Conditions
    4. DICE Analysis Step 4: Exclusions
  - E. Determination of Amounts Payable

When you take the randomized full practice exams in the SMART Online Practice Exams product, you are seeing the same kinds of questions you will see when you take the actual exam.

For each assignment, you should define or describe each of the Key Words and Phrases and answer each of the Review and Application Questions.

Educational Objective 1

Describe how individuals and families can use the Insurance Services Office, Inc., (ISO) 2011 Homeowners insurance program to address their personal risk management needs.

Key Word or Phrase

Functional replacement cost

Review Questions

1-1. Identify the three general categories into which the parties eligible for coverage under the Insurance Services Office, Inc. (ISO) 2011 Homeowners (HO) insurance program fall.

1-2. Describe the coverage provided by the HO-2 Broad Form.

1-3. Contrast the coverage provided by the HO-2 with the coverage provided by the HO-3.

1-4. Describe the coverage provided by the HO-4—Contents Broad Form.

1-5. Identify the coverage form that provides the broadest available coverage for a homeowner's home and contents.

1-6. For whose risk management needs is the HO-6—Unit-Owners Form designed?

1-7. Describe the coverage provided by the HO-8—Modified Coverage Form.

Educational Objective 2

Describe the Homeowners 3—Special Form (HO-3) in terms of:

- **Its structure and the coverages it provides**
- **The role of endorsements in modifying it**
- **The factors considered in rating it**

Review Questions

2-1. Identify the primary components of the Insurance Services Office, Inc. (ISO) Homeowners 3—Special Form (HO-3).

2-2. Give examples of questions that the declarations answer about the insured, the property covered, and the limits of coverage in the HO-3.

2-3. Explain the purpose of the HO-3 insuring agreement.

2-4. Describe the information that is included in HO-3 Section I.

2-5. Identify the ways in which endorsements can alter the HO-3.

2-6. Give examples of factors that influence the HO-3's base premium.

Educational Objective 3

Describe what is insured by each of these coverages contained in the 2011 Homeowners 3—Special Form (HO-3) policy:

- **Coverage A—Dwelling**
- **Coverage B—Other Structures**
- **Coverage C—Personal Property**
- **Coverage D—Loss of Use**
- **Additional Coverages**

Review Questions

3-1. Should an insured consider the land value at the residence premises when determining the amount of insurance to purchase under a Homeowners 3—Special Form (HO-3) policy?

3-2. Identify three exclusions to coverage in the HO-3 under Coverage B—Other Structures.

3-3. To what property does Coverage C—Personal Property apply?

3-4. Explain the purpose of the personal property special sublimits in the HO-3.

3-5. Identify why, in most cases, a particular category of coverage is excluded under Coverage C.

3-6. Name the three coverages provided under Coverage D.

3-7. Identify two reasons why some coverage is provided under the HO-3 Additional Coverages rather than under Coverage A, B, C, or D.

Application Questions

3-8. The luggage of an insured's visiting aunt is stolen from a beach house the insured has rented and occupied for a family vacation. Under what circumstances would the insured's HO-3 policy reimburse his aunt for the stolen luggage?

3-9. If a dwelling is insured under Coverage A for $400,000, for how much are the other structures on the residence premises covered?

Educational Objective 4

Describe what is covered and what is excluded by these provisions in the 2011 Homeowners 3—Special Form (HO-3) policy:

- **Perils Insured Against for Coverages A and B**
- **Perils Insured Against for Coverage C**
- **Section I—Exclusions**

Key Words and Phrases

Special form coverage

Named perils coverage

Review Questions

4-1. Explain why insured perils for Coverage A—Dwelling and Coverage B—Other Structures are grouped together in the Insurance Services Office, Inc. (ISO) Homeowners 3—Special Form (HO-3).

4-2. Describe the approach of HO-3 Section I—Property Coverages to perils insured against for direct physical loss under Coverages A and B and the intent of that approach.

4-3. Identify the type of property to which Coverage C under the HO-3 generally applies.

4-4. Explain why coverage for personal property under the HO-3 is not as broad as the open perils coverage for dwellings and other structures.

4-5. List the named perils covered under Coverage C of the HO-3 policy.

Application Questions

4-6. Julie has an HO-3 policy to insure her home, detached garage, and personal property. During a windstorm, a large tree branch fell through the roof and into Julie's living room, damaging the exterior and interior of her home, a sofa, and a coffee table. Rain that blew through the opening in the wall caused water damage to the dining room table. Considering Coverages A, B, and C, identify the appropriate coverages and explain whether the coverage(s) would insure her property against this peril (after any applicable deductible).

4-7. Assume that Julie has the same coverages as in the previous question. Julie's power company has been known to have power surges. One day, a power surge damaged Julie's central air conditioner, the components of her personal computer, and her projection television system. Identify the appropriate coverages and explain whether the coverage(s) would insure her property against this peril (after any applicable deductible).

Educational Objective 5

Summarize each of the 2011 Homeowners 3—Special Form (HO-3) policy provisions in Section I—Conditions.

Review Questions

5-1. Identify the purpose of the Insurance Services Office, Inc. (ISO) Homeowners 3—Special Form's (HO-3) Insurable Interest and Limit of Liability condition.

5-2. What was the purpose of the 2011 revision to the HO-3's Deductible condition?

5-3. List examples of the duties the insured must perform after a property loss under the HO-3.

5-4. Identify the purpose of the HO-3's Loss Settlement condition.

5-5. Summarize the procedure the HO-3's Appraisal condition outlines for resolving disputes between an insured and the insurer over the amount of a loss.

5-6. How does the HO-3 specify a loss be resolved that is covered by two or more insurance policies?

5-7. Identify the purpose of the HO-3's Our Option condition.

5-8. Describe the mortgagee rights the Mortgage Clause condition of the HO-3 establishes.

▶▶

Application Question

5-9. Kim and Dan own a home. Kim has an HO-3 with a $100,000 Coverage A limit. Dan also purchased a homeowners policy with a $150,000 Coverage A limit for the home. A natural gas explosion destroyed the couple's home, which had a replacement cost of $200,000 at the time of the loss. After the explosion, they discover that two policies cover their home, with a total of $250,000 in coverage available. Calculate the amount that each policy will pay.

Educational Objective 6

Given a scenario describing a homeowners property claim, determine whether the 2011 HO-3 policy Section I—Property Coverages would cover the claim and, if so, the amount the insurer would pay for the claim.

Application Question

6-1. Steve and Kelly own a single-family home insured under an Insurance Services Office, Inc. (ISO) Homeowners 3—Special Form (HO-3) policy. One evening, a fire destroys the home's living room and several adjoining rooms. The structural damage to the home because of the fire is $75,000. The family's television is damaged. Cash ($375), which Steve kept in a countertop cookie jar for food-shopping trips, was also destroyed. Steve and Kelly are insured under an unendorsed HO-3 policy with a $300,000 dwelling limit and a $500 deductible. For the purposes of this case, assume that Steve and Kelly are in compliance with all policy conditions, including Coverage A replacement cost provisions.

a. Identify the component of the HO-3 policy that would be used to determine whether coverage applies to Steve and Kelly at the time of the loss.

b. Identify the component of the HO-3 policy that would be used to determine whether the policy applies to Steve and Kelly's loss.

c. Steve and Kelly's HO-3 contains a provision in the Special Limits of Liability portion of its Conditions section that states that a $200 limit applies to "money." Assuming that their loss is covered under their HO-3, how, if at all, would this condition affect the amount that Steve and Kelly receive from the insurer?

d. Assuming that their loss is covered under their HO-3 and accounting for the deductible, how much will Steve and Kelly receive for fire damage to their home under Coverage A?

e. Steve and Kelly's television, destroyed in the fire, was five years old but had a useful life of ten years. A new television equivalent to the destroyed model costs $600. The insurer's claims representative determines that it would cost $400 to repair the damage. Assuming that Steve and Kelly's loss is covered under their HO-3, how would compensation for the television be settled under Coverage C?

Answers to Assignment 5 Questions

NOTE: These answers are provided to give students a basic understanding of acceptable types of responses. They often are not the only valid answers and are not intended to provide an exhaustive response to the questions.

Educational Objective 1

1-1. The three general categories into which the parties eligible for coverage under the ISO 2011 HO insurance program fall are these:

- Individuals and families who own a private home in which they reside
- People who rent or lease the premises in which they reside
- Individuals and families who own private condominium units used for residential purposes

1-2. The HO-2 Broad Form provides named perils coverage for dwellings, other structures, and personal property.

1-3. The HO-3 provides named perils coverage for personal property, as does the HO-2. The HO-3 is designed to meet the risk management needs of owner-occupants of dwellings who want broader coverage on their dwellings and other structures.

1-4. The HO-4—Contents Broad Form provides coverage for a tenant's personal property on a named perils basis.

1-5. A homeowner who desires the broadest available coverage for his or her home and contents, and is willing to pay the increased premium for it, should select the HO-5—Comprehensive Form.

1-6. The HO-6 is designed to meet the risk management needs of the owners of condominium units and cooperative apartment shares.

1-7. The HO-8—Modified Coverage Form provides coverage for a dwelling, other structures, and personal property on a limited, named perils basis.

Educational Objective 2

2-1. The HO-3 policy consists of these primary components:

- Declarations
- Agreement and Definitions
- Section I—Property Coverages
- Section II—Liability Coverages
- Endorsements

2-2. The HO-3 declarations provide essential information about the insured, the property covered, and the limits of coverage provided by answering these questions:

- Who is the policyholder?
- Where is the policyholder's residence?
- What are the coverage limits?
- What is the premium?
- What is the Section I deductible?
- What is the effective date of the policy?
- Which forms and endorsements apply to the policy?
- Who is the mortgage holder?

2-3. The purpose of the HO-3 insuring agreement is to establish the basis for the contract and specify what the insurer and the insured will do. The insurer agrees to provide coverage, and the insured agrees to pay the premium and comply with the policy conditions.

2-4. HO-3 Section I specifies the property covered, the perils for which the property is covered, and the exclusions and conditions that affect property coverages and losses.

2-5. Endorsements to the HO-3 can increase or decrease limits, add or remove coverages, change definitions, clarify policy intent, or recognize specific characteristics that require a premium increase or decrease.

2-6. Factors that influence the HO-3's base premium include dwelling location, public protection class (classification used to rate the quality of community fire protection), construction factors, coverage amount, and the policy form selected.

Educational Objective 3

3-1. An insured need not consider the land value at the residence premises because HO-3 coverage does not apply to land.

3-2. No coverage is provided for other structures that meet any of these criteria:

- A structure rented to anyone who is not a resident of the dwelling (unless it is rented as a private garage)
- A structure from which any business is conducted
- A structure used to store business property

3-3. Coverage C—Personal Property applies to items that the insured owns or uses, anywhere in the world. It can also provide coverage for personal property of others while that property is on the residence premises, if the named insured requests such coverage after a loss. Coverage C can also cover loss of or damage to personal property of a guest or residence employee while it is in any residence occupied by an insured.

3-4. The personal property special sublimits in the HO-3 limit the amount of coverage available for losses to specified items, particularly items with high value or items that may be a target for theft. The smaller limits are intended to provide adequate dollar amounts of coverage for exposures of a typical family.

3-5. In most cases, a particular category of coverage is excluded under Coverage C because the items it includes are insured through policies other than a homeowners policy.

3-6. Three coverages provided under Coverage D are these:

- Additional living expense
- Fair rental value
- Loss of use due to civil authority

3-7. Most additional coverages are given special treatment because they do not fit easily into Coverage A, B, C, or D groups. Others address items that have been excluded from the full coverage under Coverage C (such as credit cards and landlord's furnishings).

3-8. The insured's HO-3 policy would reimburse his aunt for the stolen luggage if he had elected to provide reimbursement under Coverage C for damage to or loss of personal property owned by a guest or residence employee while the property is in any residence occupied by the insured.

3-9. If a dwelling is insured under Coverage A for $400,000, the other structures on the residence premises are covered for a total of $40,000.

Educational Objective 4

4-1. Insured perils for Coverage A—Dwelling and Coverage B—Other Structures are grouped together because both coverages provide open perils coverage for real property items with similar exposures to loss.

4-2. Under the HO-3 Section I, a broad statement of coverage against direct physical loss under Coverages A and B is followed by a statement that lists the excluded perils. Any peril that is not listed in these exclusions is covered.

4-3. Coverage C under the HO-3 applies to the contents of a home and other personal property.

4-4. Coverage C applies on a named perils basis, meaning that coverage applies only if covered property is damaged as a result of a cause of loss named in the policy. While open perils and named perils cover many of the same causes of loss, open perils coverage sometimes includes causes of loss that are not among the named perils.

4-5. Coverage C named perils include these:
- Fire or lightning
- Windstorm or hail
- Explosion
- Riot or civil commotion
- Aircraft
- Vehicles
- Smoke
- Vandalism or malicious mischief
- Theft
- Falling objects
- Weight of ice, snow, or sleet
- Accidental discharge or overflow of water or steam
- Sudden and accidental tearing apart, cracking, burning, or bulging
- Freezing
- Sudden and accidental damage from artificially generated electrical current
- Volcanic eruption

4-6. Windstorm is not an excluded peril under Coverage A, so coverage would be provided for the exterior and interior damage to Julie's home. Windstorm is a named peril under Coverage C, so coverage would be provided for the damage to Julie's sofa and coffee table. Because wind (a specified peril) caused the branch to damage the structure, leaving an opening that allowed the rain into the home, the water damage to the dining room table would be covered under Coverage C.

4-7. Because no applicable exclusion exists under Coverage A, the losses to Julie's central air conditioner would be covered. Although Coverage C lists the covered peril of sudden and accidental damage from artificially generated electrical current, it makes an exception for losses to computers and home entertainment equipment. Therefore, the Coverage C losses resulting from the power surge would not be covered.

Educational Objective 5

5-1. The Insurable Interest and Limit of Liability condition limits the maximum payment for any single loss to the applicable limits shown on the Declarations page, regardless of the number of insureds who have an insurable interest in the property.

5-2. The purpose of the 2011 revision to the HO-3's Deductible condition was to reinforce the policy's intent that the deductible applies only to Section I losses.

5-3. Examples of the duties the insured must perform after a property loss under the HO-3 include these:

- Give prompt notice
- Notify the police
- Notify the credit card, electronic fund transfer card company, or access device company
- Protect the property from further damage
- Cooperate with the insurer
- Prepare an inventory
- Verify the loss
- Sign a sworn proof of loss

5-4. The Loss Settlement condition establishes the process for determining the amount to be paid for a property loss.

5-5. This is the procedure the HO-3's Appraisal condition outlines for resolving disputes between an insured and the insurer over the amount of a loss:

- The insurer and the insured each choose an appraiser to prepare an estimate of the value of the loss. Each party pays for its own appraiser.
- If the estimates differ, the two appraisers submit their differences to an umpire. The umpire is an impartial individual (often another appraiser or a judge) who resolves the differences. An agreement by any two of the three will set the amount of loss. The insurer and the insured share the cost of the umpire.

5-6. If two or more insurance policies cover the same loss, the HO-3's Other Insurance and Service Agreement condition states that the loss will be shared proportionally by all policies.

5-7. The HO-3's Our Option condition reserves the right for the insurer to repair or replace damaged property with similar property, should it choose to do so.

5-8. The mortgagee rights the Mortgage Clause condition of the HO-3 establishes are these:

- If a loss occurs to property covered by Coverage A—Dwelling or Coverage B—Other Structures, the loss is payable jointly to the mortgagee and the insured.
- A mortgagee has rights that are independent of the insured's rights. If the insurer denies the insured's loss, the mortgagee retains the right to collect from the insurer its insurable interest in the property.
- An insurer must mail notice of cancellation or nonrenewal of a policy to the mortgagee (in addition to notice sent to the insured) at least ten days before the cancellation or nonrenewal.

5-9. The insurer that issued Kim's policy will pay 40 percent of the loss ($100,000 ÷ 250,000), or $80,000 (.40 × $200,000). The insurer that issued Dan's policy will pay 60 percent of the loss ($150,000 ÷ $250,000), or $120,000 (.60 × $200,000).

Educational Objective 6

6-1. These answers are based on the facts associated with Steve and Kelly's fire case.

a. The component of the HO-3 policy that would be used to determine whether coverage would apply for Steve and Kelly at the time of the loss is the Declarations page, which specifies the named insured, the address of the covered property, and the period during which coverage applies.

b. The component of the HO-3 policy that would be used to determine whether the policy applies to Steve and Kelly's loss is the Insuring Agreement, in which the insurer agrees to pay for direct physical loss to property described in Coverages A and B (subject to certain exclusions) and for direct physical loss under Coverage C for certain named perils, including fire and subsequent smoke and water damage.

c. The $200 special limit of liability for cash would affect the amount that Steve and Kelly receive from the insurer for the money in the cookie jar that was destroyed in the fire. Instead of receiving payment for the $375 that was lost, Steve and Kelly would instead receive $200, the maximum amount allowable according to this policy condition.

d. Under Coverage A, Steve and Kelly will receive $74,500 ($75,000 less the $500 deductible) for fire damage to the home (within the $300,000 Coverage A limit) at full replacement cost, because the policy dwelling limit complies with policy replacement cost provisions.

e. Compensation for the television would be settled under Coverage C under the lesser of the television's actual cash value (ACV) at the time of the loss or the amount required to repair the television. The television's ACV can be determined by identifying what it would cost new and then subtracting a percentage of that value based on depreciation. Because the television has consumed half of its useful life, it has depreciated 50 percent. Its ACV, then, would be 50 percent of $600 ($300). Because this amount is less than the $400 it would cost to repair the damage, the claims representative would settle the loss amount for the television at $300.

Direct Your Learning

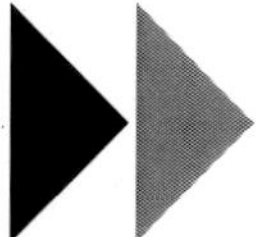

6

Homeowners Section II

Educational Objectives

After learning the content of this assignment, you should be able to:

1. Determine whether the 2011 Homeowners 3—Special Form (HO-3) policy provisions in the following Section II—Liability Coverages provide coverage for a given loss or loss exposure:
   - Coverage E—Personal Liability
   - Coverage F—Medical Payments to Others
   - Additional Coverages
2. Determine whether one or more exclusions preclude the coverage provided by Section II of the 2011 Homeowners 3—Special Form (HO-3) policy provisions in Section II—Exclusions.
3. Summarize each of these 2011 Homeowners 3—Special Form (HO-3) policy provisions:
   - Conditions applicable to Section II
   - Conditions applicable to Sections I and II
4. Compare the coverage provided by each of the following 2011 homeowners forms to the coverage provided by the 2011 Homeowners 3—Special Form (HO-3):
   - HO-2 Broad Form
   - HO-4 Contents Broad Form
   - HO-5 Comprehensive Form
   - HO-6 Unit-Owners Form
   - HO-8 Modified Coverage Form
5. Given a case describing a homeowners liability claim, determine whether the Homeowners Section II—Liability Coverages would cover the claim and, if so, the amount the insurer would pay for the claim.

Outline

- **HO-3 Section II—Liability Coverages**
  - A. Coverage E—Personal Liability
  - B. Coverage F—Medical Payments to Others
  - C. Section II—Additional Coverages
    1. Claims Expenses
    2. First Aid Expenses
    3. Damage to Property of Others
    4. Loss Assessment
- **HO-3 Section II—Exclusions**
  - A. Motor Vehicle and Other Motorized Craft—Exclusions
    1. Motor Vehicle Liability
    2. Watercraft Liability
    3. Aircraft and Hovercraft Liability
  - B. Coverage E—Personal Liability and Coverage F—Medical Payments to Others
    1. Expected or Intended Injury
    2. Business
    3. Other Coverage E and Coverage F Exclusions
  - C. Exclusions That Apply Only to Coverage E
  - D. Exclusions That Apply Only to Coverage F
- **HO-3 Section II—Conditions**
  - A. Conditions Applicable to Section II
    1. Limit of Liability
    2. Severability of Insurance
    3. Duties After "Occurrence"
    4. Duties of an Injured Person—Coverage F—Medical Payments to Others
    5. Payment of Claim—Coverage F—Medical Payments to Others
    6. Suit Against Us
    7. Additional Section II Conditions
  - B. Conditions Applicable to Sections I and II
    1. Liberalization Clause
    2. Waiver or Change of Policy Provisions
    3. Cancellation
    4. Nonrenewal
    5. Assignment
    6. Subrogation
    7. Death
- **Coverage Variations in ISO Homeowners Forms**
  - A. HO-2 Broad Form Compared With HO-3
  - B. HO-4 Contents Broad Form Compared With HO-3
  - C. HO-5 Comprehensive Form Compared With HO-3
  - D. HO-6 Unit-Owners Form Compared With HO-3
  - E. HO-8 Modified Coverage Form Compared With HO-3
- **Determining Whether Homeowners Section II—Liability Coverages Covers a Claim**
  - A. Case Facts
  - B. Necessary Reference Materials
  - C. Overview of Steps
  - D. Determination of Coverage
    1. DICE Analysis Step 1: Declarations
    2. DICE Analysis Step 2: Insuring Agreement
    3. DICE Analysis Step 3: Conditions
  - E. DICE Analysis Step 4: Exclusions
  - F. Determination of Amounts Payable

When reviewing for your exam, remember to allot time for frequent breaks.

For each assignment, you should define or describe each of the Key Words and Phrases and answer each of the Review and Application Questions.

Educational Objective 1

Determine whether the 2011 Homeowners 3—Special Form (HO-3) policy provisions in the following Section II—Liability Coverages provide coverage for a given loss or loss exposure:

- **Coverage E—Personal Liability**
- **Coverage F—Medical Payments to Others**
- **Additional Coverages**

Key Words and Phrases

Third party

Bodily injury

Property damage

Occurrence

Review Questions

1-1. Explain when the insurer's obligation to defend an insured under Homeowners 3—Special Form (HO-3) Section II Coverage E ends.

1-2. Describe the coverage that is provided and the expenses that are paid under HO-3 Section II Coverage F—Medical Payments to Others.

1-3. Describe how Medical Payments to Others coverage differs from bodily injury liability coverage also provided by Section II.

1-4. List the claims expenses that an insurer may pay under Section II—Additional Coverage on the insured's behalf in addition to any judgment or settlement.

1-5. Describe the types of losses that are covered under the Loss Assessment additional coverage of the HO-3 policy.

Application Question

1-6. Dave has an HO-3 policy to insure his home, personal property, and liability. He shares his home with his ten-year-old son, James. For each of these situations, explain whether coverage would be provided under Coverage E—Personal Liability, Coverage F—Medical Payments to Others, or Section II—Additional Coverages (such as Claim Expense, First Aid Expenses, Damage to Property of Others, or Loss Assessment).

a. The family's one-year-old German shepherd, which often escapes from its enclosure, ran into their neighbor's yard and attacked their neighbor's three-year-old daughter. She suffered serious bite wounds on her face and arms.

b. James invited his friend Timmy to their home to play catch under Dave's supervision. Timmy tossed the ball straight up, intending to catch it. However, the ball hit Timmy in the face, breaking his glasses and cutting his cheek. Dave used a bandage and an ice pack from his first-aid kit to treat Timmy's injuries and then called Timmy's parents. Timmy's cut required stitches and resulted in $700 in medical expenses.

c. Dave was required to join a homeowners association when he bought his home. The association owns a clubhouse. A guest at the clubhouse became permanently disabled after he fell down the stairs. The loss settlement for the claim exceeded the liability limit of the association's policy, so each member was assessed $5,000.

d. Dave borrowed his brother's golf cart for a weekend golf tournament. While his friend Sam was riding in the cart, Dave stopped the cart on a hill and jumped out. However, he failed to properly set the parking brake. The cart rolled down the hill hitting a tree, damaging the cart. Sam jumped out of the cart before it hit the tree but hurt his shoulder when he hit the ground. His shoulder required medical attention. His emergency room bill was $300. Sam is only seeking reimbursement of his medical bills.

Educational Objective 2

Determine whether one or more exclusions preclude the coverage provided by Section II of the 2011 Homeowners 3—Special Form (HO-3) policy provisions in Section II—Exclusions.

Key Word or Phrase

Loss assessment

Review Questions

2-1. Describe the first four exclusions of the Homeowners 3—Special Form (HO-3) policy Section II that apply to losses arising from motor vehicles, watercraft, aircraft, and hovercraft.

2-2. Explain what the HO-3 Section II Motor Vehicle Exclusion is designed to do.

2-3. Describe the Expected or Intended Injury exclusion that applies to HO-3 Coverages E and F.

2-4. Describe the three exceptions to the HO-3 Section II Business exclusion that allow for some common rental situations.

2-5. Describe the two types of written contracts that are exceptions to the HO-3 Section II Coverage E Personal Liability exclusion, which eliminates coverage for liability assumed under contract or agreement.

Application Question

2-6. Paul and Terri own a home with a four-stall detached garage and insure it under an HO-3 policy. Their eight-year-old daughter, Stacy, lives with them, as does Holly, their twenty-eight-year-old nanny. The couple's state law requires that homeowners provide workers compensation benefits for domestic workers. For each of these situations, explain which of the HO-3 Section II Exclusions should be considered and whether the exclusions affect the HO-3 coverage.

a. Stacy sold lemonade from a stand along her street one hot afternoon and inadvertently added a harmful liquid to the product. A customer required a trip to the emergency room for treatment immediately after drinking the tainted lemonade.

b. Paul rents a stall of his garage to his neighbor for her private auto for $40 per month during the winter.

c. Terri is an accountant and prepares income taxes for personal clients each year in her spare time. Terri miscalculated some figures on a tax return she prepared for a client. The error was not found until several years later. The client was required to pay penalties and interest to the federal government.

d. While she was off duty, Holly went to a movie downtown with a friend. After crossing the street by the theater, Holly tripped on the curb and sprained her ankle.

Educational Objective 3

Summarize each of these 2011 Homeowners 3—Special Form (HO-3) policy provisions:

- **Conditions applicable to Section II**
- **Conditions applicable to Sections I and II**

Key Words and Phrases

Severability of Insurance condition

Waiver

Apparent authority

Binding authority

Review Questions

3-1. As described in the Homeowners 3—Special Form (HO-3) Section II Limit of Liability condition, explain how the limits of Coverage E—Personal Liability and of Coverage F—Medical Payments to Others on the Declarations page apply when numerous people are injured in the same occurrence.

3-2. Explain the operation of the Severability of Insurance condition under Section II of the HO-3 in conjunction with the limit of liability.

3-3. Under the HO-3 Section II—Conditions, what are the insured's duties after an occurrence?

3-4. Describe the Payment of Claim condition under HO-3 Coverage F.

3-5. Explain how the HO-3 Section II Concealment or Fraud condition would apply to an insured who was not involved in the concealment or fraud.

3-6. Explain why courts have permitted use of oral waivers by claims representatives made during the adjustment of a loss and after issuance of the written policy.

Application Questions

3-7. Anthony has an HO-3 policy to insure his home, personal property, and liability. He shares his home with his aunt Mabel, who is an insured under the policy. For each of these situations, explain any applicable conditions and how the coverage would be affected.

a. Mabel's dog escaped one afternoon and entered a nearby grocery store, where he was inadvertently shut in a cooler. The dog destroyed several cases of frozen meat and other goods and damaged the shelving before the grocery staff found him. Mabel retrieved her dog, and the grocery store filed a suit against Mabel and Anthony, individually, for $8,000 each in damages for the loss of product and the loss of use of the cooler. When the legal documents arrived, Mabel notified the insurer of the claim circumstances and forwarded her documents to the insurer, but Anthony failed to forward his legal documents. The grocery store won the suit against Mabel and Anthony. The court found Mabel liable for $8,000 in damages and Anthony liable for $8,000.

b. Anthony invited a friend, Trisha, into his home. Trisha tripped over Mabel's dog, fell through a glass patio door, and required medical treatment that cost $850. Anthony gave written notice to his insurer of the occurrence the following morning. The insurer offered to pay Trisha's medical expenses under Coverage F—Medical Payments to Others.

c. An elderly friend of Mabel's, Esther, tripped on a loose board and fell down the front steps of Anthony's home. Esther broke her hip and was hospitalized for four months, incurring medical expenses of $9,000. Anthony gave written notice to his insurer of the occurrence the following day. Before Esther's treatment was completed, Anthony filed for bankruptcy. The insurer offered to pay $1,000 of Esther's medical expenses under Coverage F—Medical Payments to Others.

3-8. One month after renewing their homeowners insurance policy, Charlotte and Allan sold their home to another couple, Laura and Luke, who had relocated from another state. To make life a little easier for Laura and Luke, Charlotte and Allan decided to transfer their homeowners insurance to them. Explain whether the transfer is legally enforceable.

Educational Objective 4

Compare the coverage provided by each of the following 2011 homeowners forms to the coverage provided by the 2011 Homeowners 3—Special Form (HO-3):

- **HO-2 Broad Form**
- **HO-4 Contents Broad Form**
- **HO-5 Comprehensive Form**
- **HO-6 Unit-Owners Form**
- **HO-8 Modified Coverage Form**

Key Words and Phrases

Condominium

Cooperative corporation

Review Questions

4-1. Describe four situations that the Insurance Services Office, Inc. (ISO) homeowners forms other than the Homeowners 3—Special Form (HO-3) are intended to address.

4-2. Identify the section of the HO-3 and the other homeowners forms that contains the primary differences between the forms.

4-3. Both the Homeowners 2—Broad Form (HO-2) and the HO-3 are designed for owner-occupants of a house. Explain why a homeowner would choose to use the HO-2 instead of the HO-3.

4-4. Explain how the burden of proof for losses under named perils coverage differs from the burden of proof for losses under special form coverage.

4-5. Explain the coverage need that the Homeowners 4—Contents Broad Form (HO-4) is designed to fill.

Application Questions

4-6. Janet bought a condominium. The condominium declaration or master deed for her condominium association requires the association to purchase insurance to cover only the "bare walls," which applies only to the building structure and walls that support the structure. Janet bought a Homeowners 6—Unit-Owners Form (HO-6) policy to cover her unit, personal property, and liability. After her purchase, but before she moved in with her belongings, an electrical fire damaged exterior walls, light fixtures, plumbing fixtures, wiring, and a partition in her unit. Repair estimates indicate it will cost $2,000 to repair damage to the exterior walls and $4,000 to fix the remaining damage. The repairs will take one month, during which time the unit will be uninhabitable. Assuming no deductible applies, what coverage will be available under Janet's HO-6 policy for her loss?

4-7. Jim and Ann purchased an older home in the historic section of their town for a low price. The home has many unique features, including carved wood doors, a spiral staircase, and antique light fixtures that would be expensive to replace if the home sustained major damage. Which homeowners policy would be appropriate for the loss exposures for this home? Explain.

Educational Objective 5

Given a case describing a homeowners liability claim, determine whether the Homeowners Section II—Liability Coverages would cover the claim and, if so, the amount the insurer would pay for the claim.

Application Question

5-1. Tom and Sandy have an Insurance Services Office, Inc. (ISO) Homeowners 3—Special Form (HO-3) policy covering their home. The policy has Section II Coverage E—Personal Liability with a limit of $500,000 for each occurrence and Coverage F—Medical Payments to Others with a limit of $5,000 for each person. Both Tom and Sandy are listed as named insureds on the policy, and the annual policy has been in effect for six months. Their five-year-old son, Johnny, resides with them. Recently, Sandy's friend Cathy came over to the residence for a card game. Cathy tripped over one of Johnny's toys and suffered a compound fracture in one of her legs, requiring emergency surgery. As a result of her injury, she incurred $20,000 in medical expenses. Moreover, she was unable to work for four months and incurred $30,000 in lost wages. Cathy has made a claim against Tom and Sandy alleging that they are legally liable to pay the damages resulting from the injury she sustained in their home. Tom and Sandy promptly reported the accident to their insurer and are cooperating in the insurer's investigation. Assuming that Tom and Sandy are legally liable for Cathy's damages, will Tom and Sandy's HO-3 cover Cathy's claim? If so, what amount will the insurer pay for the claim? When determining whether coverage applies to the losses, you can apply the four steps of the DICE method. ("DICE" stands for declarations, insuring agreement, conditions, and exclusions.)

a. The first DICE step is to review the policy's declarations page to determine whether the individuals are covered, the location is covered, and the incident occurred during the policy period.

b. The second DICE step is to determine whether the event triggers coverage under an insuring agreement in Section II of the HO-3 policy.

c. The third DICE step is to determine whether all policy conditions have been met.

d. The fourth DICE step is to determine whether one or more exclusions preclude coverage that the insuring agreements have granted.

e. Now that you have completed the DICE analysis, you can determine the amounts payable.

Answers to Assignment 6 Questions

NOTE: These answers are provided to give students a basic understanding of acceptable types of responses. They often are not the only valid answers and are not intended to provide an exhaustive response to the questions.

Educational Objective 1

1-1. The insurer's obligation to defend ends only when the liability limit for the occurrence is exhausted by payment of a settlement or judgment (even if policy limits are exhausted by the costs of the claim).

1-2. Coverage F—Medical Payments to Others covers medical payments incurred by others (not insureds or regular household residents) under certain conditions within three years of an injury. These medical expenses include reasonable charges for medical, surgical, x-ray, dental, ambulance, hospital, professional nursing, and funeral services, and prosthetic devices. This limit is generally set at $1,000 per person for a single accident.

1-3. Medical Payments to Others coverage may be considered to overlap with bodily injury liability coverage. However, liability coverage applies only when an insured is legally responsible for damages. Claims for medical payments are often paid when the insured feels a moral obligation to another person, even though the insured is not negligent or legally responsible. When a bodily injury claim involves a relatively small amount of money, paying it as a Medical Payments to Others claim simplifies matters by eliminating any need to determine whether an insured was legally responsible for the injuries.

1-4. These Additional Coverage expenses may be paid on the insured's behalf:

- Expenses the insurer incurs
- Premiums on bonds
- Reasonable expenses
- Postjudgment interest

1-5. The Loss Assessment additional coverage provides up to $1,000 for an insured's share of a loss assessment charged to the insured by a corporation or an association of property owners for these types of losses:

- Bodily injury or property damage that is not excluded under Section II of the homeowners policy
- Liability that results from an act of an elected and unpaid director, officer, or trustee

1-6. These answers address questions regarding Dave's HO-3 case study:

a. Coverage F will provide $1,000 medical payments coverage for the girl's injuries. Coverage E will provide liability coverage for the girl's injuries and damages, assuming Dave is legally liable. If the neighbors sue Dave, Coverage E will pay his defense costs until the liability limit for the occurrence is exhausted by payment of a settlement or judgment. Section II—Additional Coverages will cover certain claims expenses related to any lawsuit that ensued in addition to any settlement or judgment.

b. Coverage F will pay the $700 in medical expenses because Timmy was an invited guest and the injury was accidental. Because Timmy is responsible for his own injury and Dave was properly supervising the children when the accident occurred, he probably would not be liable for the damages and Coverage E would not be needed. However, Section II—Additional Coverages will reimburse Dave for the first-aid supplies he used. These payments can be made without litigation and the need to determine fault.

c. The Loss Assessment provision under Section II—Additional Coverages will pay $1,000 for Dave's share of the loss assessment.

d. Coverage E will pay for the property damage to Dave's brother's cart. Coverage F will pay up to $1,000 for Sam's medical expenses. Coverage E is also available for Sam's bodily injury loss, if needed.

Educational Objective 2

2-1. These are the first four exclusions of HO-3 Section II that apply to losses arising from motor vehicles, watercraft, aircraft, and hovercraft:

- The ownership, maintenance, occupancy, operation, use, loading, or unloading of a motor vehicle or craft by any person unless it appears in a specific exception to the exclusion
- Negligent entrustment, by an insured, of an excluded motor vehicle or craft
- An insured's failure to supervise, or negligence in supervising, a person
- An insured's "vicarious liability" for the actions of a child or minor

2-2. The HO-3 Section II Motor Vehicle Liability exclusion is designed to limit the majority of personal motor vehicle loss exposures that would typically be insured under a Personal Auto Policy (PAP).

2-3. The HO-3 Section II Expected or Intended Injury exclusion applies to any bodily injury or property damage caused by an insured when the bodily injury or property damage is intentional or expected, even if the actual injury or damage resulting from the action was unintended when the intentional action took place.

2-4. These are the three exceptions to the HO-3 Section II Business exclusion that allow for some common rental situations:

- Rental of an insured location on an occasional basis is a covered loss exposure if the location is used only as a residence.
- Rental of part of an insured location as a residence is a covered loss exposure, as long as the occupying family takes no more than two roomers or boarders in a single-family unit.
- Rental of part of an insured location is a covered loss exposure if it is used only as an office or a school, studio, or private garage.

2-5. The two types of written contracts that are exceptions to the HO-3 Section II Coverage E—Personal Liability exclusion, which eliminates coverage for liability assumed under contract or agreement, are these:

- Contracts relating to the ownership, maintenance, or use of an insured location
- Contracts relating to the liability of others assumed by the named insured before an accident occurs

2-6. These answers address questions regarding the HO-3 Exclusions case study:

a. The Coverage E and F Business exclusion could be considered. However, the Business exclusion is designed to exclude coverage for bodily injury or property damage arising out of business activities of an insured while providing coverage for occasional or part-time activities, such as insureds under the age of twenty-one selling lemonade. Another exception involves activities for which the insured receives $2,000 or less during the year preceding the policy period, which likely applies to Stacy's lemonade stand operations. So liability coverage applies.

b. The Coverage E and F Business exclusion could be considered. However, liability for rental as a private garage is an exception to the exclusion. So coverage is provided.

c. The Coverage E and F Professional Services exclusion could be considered. The exclusion would apply to Terri's tax preparation business, for which her liability should be covered under a professional liability policy. Therefore, no coverage applies under the HO-3 policy.

d. The Coverage F Residence Employee Off Premises exclusion and the Coverage E Bodily Injury to Persons Eligible for Workers Compensation Benefits exclusion should be considered. The Residence Employee Off Premises—Coverage F excludes bodily injury to a residence employee if the injury occurs off the insured's location and the injury does not arise out of the employee's work. Holly was off the insured's location and off duty at the time of the injury, so the exclusion applies. In addition, the Bodily Injury to Persons Eligible for Workers Compensation Benefits—Coverage E excludes coverage for Holly for her bodily injury because she is eligible to receive benefits as an insured under her state's workers compensation law. So no coverage applies under the HO-3 policy.

Educational Objective 3

3-1. The Section II Limit of Liability provision stipulates that the limit of Coverage E—Personal Liability appearing on the Declarations page is the total limit of coverage for any one occurrence. This limit does not increase, regardless of the number of insureds, claims made, or people injured. This condition further states that the limit of liability applicable to Coverage F—Medical Payments to Others for all medical expenses for bodily injury to one person as the result of an accident cannot exceed the Coverage F limit shown on the Declarations page. The Coverage F limit can apply to more than one person per accident.

3-2. Under the Severability of Insurance condition, each insured seeking protection is treated as if he or she has separate coverage under the policy. However, the insurer's limit of liability stated in the policy is not increased for any one occurrence if more than one insured is involved.

3-3. The insured's duties after an occurrence include these requirements:

- Give written notice to the insurer as soon as practical.
- Cooperate with the insurer's investigation, settlement, and defense activities.
- Forward legal documents promptly to the insurer.
- Provide claims assistance to the insurer in making a settlement, enforcing any right of contribution against another party, attending hearings and trials, securing and giving evidence, and obtaining the attendance of witnesses.
- Submit evidence for damage to property of others when a claim is made under the additional coverage for damage to property of others; the insured must submit to the insurer a sworn statement of loss and show the damaged property to the insurer.
- Do not make voluntary payment; if the insured does so, it will be at the insured's own expense.

3-4. The Coverage F Payment of Claim condition stipulates that the insurer's payment of a Medical Payments to Others claim is not an admission of liability by the insured or the insurer. The intent of Section II medical payments coverage is to prevent suits or to reduce the damages resulting from possible claims by providing prompt payment for injured parties' medical expenses without the need to determine fault.

3-5. The Concealment or Fraud condition excludes coverage only for the insured(s) involved in the concealment or fraud, or those making false statements. Other innocent insureds would not be excluded from liability coverage.

3-6. Courts have permitted use of oral waivers by claims representatives made during the adjustment of a loss and after the written policy was issued because claims representatives are the insurer's representatives and have apparent authority to modify policy conditions.

3-7. These answers address questions regarding the Anthony and Mabel case study:

a. Two conditions could affect coverage under Section II Coverage E of Anthony's policy—the Duties After "Occurrence" and the Severability of Insurance conditions. Because Mabel is an insured, coverage is provided under the policy for her liability. Mabel complied with the conditions specified for Duties After "Occurrence," so coverage would be provided for Mabel's liability of $8,000 up to the policy limits. But Anthony did not comply with the duties, which hindered the insurer in performing its duties. Consequently, the insurer is not obligated to pay Anthony's liability under the policy. The Severability of Insurance condition allows Mabel to be treated as if she has separate coverage under the policy, so the insurer's denial of payment for Anthony's liability would not affect its payment of Mabel's liability. Anthony could be held personally responsible for the $8,000 liability settlement against him. Finally, the Suit Against Us condition could bar Anthony from suing his insurer for failure to pay the judgment because he did not meet all of his obligations under Section II of the policy.

b. To obtain medical payments coverage, Trisha must comply with all requirements under the Duties of an Injured Person condition of Coverage F. The Payment of Claim condition also applies here, stipulating that the insurer's payment of Trisha's Medical Payments to Others claim is not an admission of liability for the occurrence. Anthony complied with the Duties After "Occurrence" condition, so coverage was provided.

c. Because Anthony complied with the Duties After "Occurrence" condition, coverage was available under the policy. To obtain Medical Payments coverage, Esther must comply with the Duties of an Injured Person condition of Coverage F, and the Payment of Claim condition would specify that the payment was not an admission of liability. Even though Anthony filed bankruptcy, the Bankruptcy of an Insured condition still obligated the insurer to pay Esther's bodily injury claim under Coverage E—Personal Liability.

3-8. Charlotte and Allan's transfer of their homeowners policy to Laura and Luke may not be legally enforceable, because an insurance policy is a personal contract between the insurer and the policyholder. Therefore, the insurer is able to choose whom it will insure. The assignment condition states that any assignment of the policy will not be valid unless the insurer provides its written consent.

Educational Objective 4

4-1. ISO homeowners forms other than the HO-3 are intended to address situations such as these:

- Apartment dwellers and condominium unit owners who do not need full insurance on the buildings in which they live
- Customers who will accept more restricted coverage than the HO-3 provides in exchange for lower premiums
- Customers who are willing to pay for the broadest coverage possible
- Older homes that have depreciated substantially and are not well-suited for the replacement cost coverage provided by the HO-3

4-2. The primary differences between the HO-3 and the other homeowners forms are in each form's Section I—Property Coverages. The Agreement, Section II—Liability Coverages, and Section II—Conditions are identical in all ISO homeowners forms.

4-3. A homeowner might choose to use the HO-2 instead of the HO-3 because the HO-2 has a lower premium than the HO-3. This is because it covers the dwelling and other structures against fewer causes of loss. In the HO-2, covered causes of loss are limited to the named perils listed in the policy, not only for personal property but also for the building and other structures.

4-4. With named perils coverage, such as the HO-2, the insured must prove the loss was caused by a covered cause of loss for coverage to apply. The burden of proof is on the insured. With special form coverage, if a loss to covered property occurs, the initial assumption is that it is covered. To deny coverage, the insurer must prove the loss was caused by an excluded cause of loss. The burden of proof in this case is on the insurer.

4-5. The HO-4 is designed for the needs of people who live in rented houses or apartments.

4-6. Coverage A—Dwelling of Janet's HO-6 policy provides a basic limit of $5,000. The repair bill of $4,000 is payable by her insurer. The $2,000 to repair the exterior walls should be covered by the condominium association insurance. Also, because Janet had not yet moved in her personal property, it is likely that Coverage C—Personal Property of her policy will not be needed. However, Coverage D—Loss of Use should be helpful. Janet's unit will be uninhabitable until the repairs are complete, which is estimated to take one month. During that time, Janet will have to find another place to live. Coverage D will pay the cost to rent this other place. Coverage D is limited to 50 percent of Coverage C.

4-7. A Homeowners 8—Modified Coverage Form (HO-8) policy would be a logical choice for Jim and Ann because replacement of the unique features as a result of a covered cause of loss would likely exceed the market value of the house. When the market value is substantially lower than the replacement cost, the situation creates an obvious moral hazard, and Jim and Ann's insurer may be unwilling to cover them with any other form. The HO-8 addresses this potential problem under Section I—Conditions. A provision in this section specifies that if the insured makes repairs after a loss, the insurer will not pay more than the cost of "common construction materials and methods" that are "functionally equivalent to and less costly than obsolete, antique, or custom construction."

Educational Objective 5

5-1. These answers relate to the Tom and Sandy case:

a. In this case, the policy lists Tom and Sandy as named insureds, and the accident occurred at their residence during the policy period.

b. Cathy's liability claim against Tom and Sandy triggers coverage under the Coverage E—Personal Liability insuring agreement because her claim alleges damages because of bodily injury for which Tom and Sandy are legally liable. Cathy's broken leg qualifies as bodily injury and Tom and Sandy both meet the policy definition of insured. Cathy's medical expenses (but not her loss of wages or pain and suffering) could also be covered under the Coverage F—Medical Payments to Others insurance agreement (up to the $5,000 limit). However, because Cathy has made a liability claim against Tom and Sandy, the claim will be handled under the Coverage E insuring agreement only.

c. The relevant policy conditions include promptly notifying the insurer of the loss and assisting the insurer as requested in its investigation. Tom and Sandy have fulfilled both of these conditions.

d. Based on the case facts, no exclusions apply to this accident.

e. The insurer will pay Cathy's medical expenses ($20,000), her lost wages ($30,000), and whatever sum is either negotiated in a settlement with the insurer or awarded by a court for her pain and suffering. If Cathy's pain and suffering is determined to be $5,000, the insurer would pay a total of $55,000 in damages, which is less than the Coverage E limit. Any costs incurred to defend Tom and Sandy against Cathy's suit would be payable in full, not subject to the limit of insurance.

Direct Your Learning

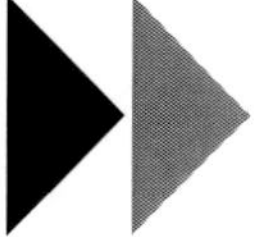

7

Using Homeowners Endorsements to Meet Individual Needs

Educational Objectives

After learning the content of this assignment, you should be able to:

1. For each of the homeowners policy endorsements for modifying limits and adding special deductibles, explain when each endorsement is needed or used and how the endorsement modifies the homeowners form to which it is attached.
2. For each of the homeowners policy endorsements for modifying the perils insured against, explain when each endorsement is needed or used and how the endorsement modifies the homeowners form to which it is attached.
3. For each of the homeowners policy endorsements for modifying property valuation provisions, explain when each endorsement is needed or used and how the endorsement modifies the homeowners form to which it is attached.
4. For each of the homeowners policy endorsements for insuring business exposures, explain when each endorsement is needed or used and how the endorsement modifies the homeowners form to which it is attached.
5. For each of the homeowners policy endorsements for insuring rental exposures, explain when each endorsement is needed or used and how the endorsement modifies the homeowners form to which it is attached.
6. For each of the homeowners policy endorsements for addressing miscellaneous exposures, explain when each endorsement is needed or used and how the endorsement modifies the homeowners form to which it is attached.
7. Given a description of an individual's or a family's loss exposures, recommend an appropriate homeowners form and endorsements for covering those exposures.

Outline

- Homeowners Endorsements for Modifying Limits and Adding Special Deductibles
- Homeowners Endorsements for Modifying Perils Insured Against
- Homeowners Endorsements for Modifying Valuation Provisions
- Homeowners Endorsements for Insuring Business Exposures
- Homeowners Endorsements for Insuring Rental Exposures
- Homeowners Endorsements for Addressing Miscellaneous Exposures
- Recommending Homeowners Forms and Endorsements
  - A. Young Family on a Tight Budget
    - 1. Recommendations for Fred and Colleen
  - B. Artist's Apartment and Studio
    - 1. Recommendations for Mark
  - C. Wealthy Married Couple
    - 1. Recommendations for Stan and Peggy
  - D. Married Couple With Home Business and Rental Property
    - 1. Recommendations for Rick and Marie
  - E. Professor's Condominium Unit
    - 1. Recommendations for Sheila

Find complete information regarding exam dates and fees at www.TheInstitutes.org/forms. Plan to register with The Institutes well in advance of your exam. If you have any questions, or need updated registration information, contact The Institutes.

For each assignment, you should define or describe each of the Key Words and Phrases and answer each of the Review and Application Questions.

Educational Objective 1

For each of the homeowners policy endorsements for modifying limits and adding special deductibles, explain when each endorsement is needed or used and how the endorsement modifies the homeowners form to which it is attached.

Review Questions

1-1. Explain how Coverage C is affected by Additional Limits of Liability for Coverages A, B, C and D (HO 04 11) when only a loss to personal property occurs.

1-2. Describe how an endorsement can increase Coverage C for personal property stored at a residence other than the residence premises.

1-3. Describe the advantage of using the percentage deductible in the Windstorm or Hail Percentage Deductible endorsement (HO 03 12) over a flat deductible.

Application Question

1-4. Doug inherited a collection of ten rare coins. Each coin is valued between $500 and $750. Describe how an endorsement can provide additional coverage that Doug may want.

Educational Objective 2

For each of the homeowners policy endorsements for modifying the perils insured against, explain when each endorsement is needed or used and how the endorsement modifies the homeowners form to which it is attached.

Review Questions

2-1. Explain what coverage in a homeowners endorsement is available to an insured who wants to insure computer equipment on an open peril basis.

2-2. Describe how the earthquake deductible is determined in the Earthquake endorsement (HO 04 54).

2-3. Describe the definition of sink hole collapse used in the Sinkhole Collapse endorsement (HO 04 99).

Application Question

2-4. Sarah has accumulated several expensive collector's postage stamps that she wants insured on an open perils basis. What coverage is available by endorsement to her homeowners policy?

Educational Objective 3

For each of the homeowners policy endorsements for modifying property valuation provisions, explain when each endorsement is needed or used and how the endorsement modifies the homeowners form to which it is attached.

Review Questions

3-1. Explain what an insurer can do if it wants to limit loss settlement on all covered property to actual cash value.

3-2. Describe what amount an insurer will pay using the Personal Property Replacement Cost Loss Settlement endorsement (HO 04 90).

3-3. Describe an endorsement the owner of an old home may want to consider.

Application Question

3-4. George had an accidental fire in the kitchen of his home. He learned from that experience that if a fire were to occur in his home again, his insurer, depending on the amount of depreciation assessed, may not pay him nearly enough to replace his carpet or household appliances that become damaged as a result of a fire. Is there coverage available to help George avoid such a large out-of-pocket expense?

Educational Objective 4

For each of the homeowners policy endorsements for insuring business exposures, explain when each endorsement is needed or used and how the endorsement modifies the homeowners form to which it is attached.

Review Questions

4-1. Explain what an insurer can do if its underwriter does not want to provide personal and advertising injury liability coverage to an insured who has started a business in his home, has added Home Business Insurance Coverage endorsement (HO 07 01) to his homeowners policy, and has a history of incurring a higher-than-average number of personal injury claims.

4-2. Describe what endorsement is available to an insured that conducts incidental dance lessons at her home.

4-3. Describe what endorsement is available to insureds that run home day cares business in their homes.

Application Question

4-4. Two friends, Bob and Dave, decided to open an auto repair shop in the house where Bob lives by himself. They heard from a neighbor there was an endorsement Bob could add to his homeowners policy that would provide most, if not all, of the business insurance coverage they would need. Explain what problems the two friends may run into in terms of insurance coverage.

Educational Objective 5

For each of the homeowners policy endorsements for insuring rental exposures, explain when each endorsement is needed or used and how the endorsement modifies the homeowners form to which it is attached.

Review Questions

5-1. Describe circumstances under which the Extended Theft Coverage for Residence Premises Occasionally Rented to Others endorsement (HO 05 41) is not needed by an insured who occasionally rents the residence premises in whole or in part to a tenant.

5-2. Describe how the Unit-Owners Rental to Others endorsement (HO 17 33) modifies Coverage C.

5-3. Describe how an insured who owns an additional residence and rents it to others continuously can obtain property insurance when the residence is ineligible for a HO policy because it is not owner occupied.

Application Question

5-4. Samantha has acquired several single-family residences that she rents to tenants continuously. Can she obtain liability coverage through her HO policy?

Educational Objective 6

For each of the homeowners policy endorsements for addressing miscellaneous exposures, explain when each endorsement is needed or used and how the endorsement modifies the homeowners form to which it is attached.

Review Questions

6-1. Describe the homeowners policy endorsement that is available to extend coverage to a relative who regularly resides in an assisted living facility.

6-2. Explain what liability coverages are available to an insured who buys a watercraft with one or more outboard engines or motors of more than twenty-five total horsepower.

6-3. Describe what offenses can be covered by the Personal Injury Coverage endorsement (HO 24 82).

Application Question

6-4. Harry bought a snowmobile, which he rides on his property around his house, but he wants to ride it on trails in local parks. What liability coverage is available for Harry from his homeowner's policy for using his snowmobile on trails?

Educational Objective 7

Given a description of an individual's or a family's loss exposures, recommend an appropriate homeowners form and endorsements for covering those exposures.

Application Question

7-1. John and Cynthia are a married couple who are insured under a standard Insurance Services Office, Inc. (ISO) Homeowners 3—Special Form (HO-3) policy without any coverage endorsements attached. John is a talented musician who plays for fun with a band that occasionally performs at public events for no fee. He keeps his musical instruments and sound equipment, valued at $40,000, in his home. His favorite instrument—which he uses in most of his performances—is an acoustic bass fiddle given to him by his uncle fifteen years ago. John wants his instruments to be covered on an open perils basis with broad coverage for breakage. Moreover, because the actual cash value of John's bass fiddle is significantly less than its replacement cost value, John wants his instruments to be covered for their full replacement cost.

Cynthia owns and operates a home-based floral business specializing in weddings. Before a major job, Cynthia can have over $5,000 of perishable flowers in her refrigerators, and power outages are common in her locality.

John and Cynthia have remodeled their garage as a furnished apartment that they rent to college students. The value of the furnishings is $10,000. John and Cynthia want to make sure that their homeowners policy provides property and liability coverage for the rented structure, including the full value of its furnishings.

Recommend endorsements for these exposures:

a. John's musical instruments and equipment

b. Cynthia's business exposures

c. Exposures related to renting the garage

Answers to Assignment 7 Questions

NOTE: These answers are provided to give students a basic understanding of acceptable types of responses. They often are not the only valid answers and are not intended to provide an exhaustive response to the questions.

Educational Objective 1

1-1. The endorsement would not activate an increase in the Coverage C limit.

1-2. The Pesonal Property at Other Residences endorsement (HO 04 50) can increase the limit for Coverage C that covers personal property usually located in a residence other than the residence premises and the value of the property exceeds 10% of the Coverage C limit or $1,000, whichever is greater.

1-3. In contrast with a flat deductible, a percentage deductible increases in proportion to the dollar amount of the loss. This approach makes it more feasible for insurers to accept properties in areas that have catastrophic wind or hail potential.

1-4. Unendorsed, Doug's policy will pay no more than $250 for any one coin and only $1,000 for Doug's entire coin collection. Using the Scheduled Personal Property Endorsement (HO 04 61), Doug can schedule the higher amount of coverage needed for each coin.

Educational Objective 2

2-1. If the insured does not already have open perils coverage on personal property, Special Computer Coverage (HO 04 14) will cover computer hardware, software, operating systems, networks, and peripherals on an open perils basis.

2-2. The earthquake deductible is determined by multiplying either the Coverage A or Coverage C limit (whichever is greater) by the deductible percentage amount shown in the schedule. In no event will the deductible be less than $500.

2-3. The Sinkhole Collapse Endorsement (HO 04 99) defines sinkhole collapse as physical damage caused by sudden settlement or collapse of the earth supporting the property. "The settlement or collapse must result from subterranean voids created by the action of water on limestone or similar rock formations."

2-4. Scheduled Personal Property Endorsement (HO 04 61) provides the open perils coverage for Sarah's postage stamps that she requested. The scheduled categories or items of eligible property are covered on an open perils basis without several exclusions that normally apply to open perils coverage. For example, breakage of the covered property is covered without the usual requirement that the breakage must be caused by a specified peril such as fire. However, Sarah should be aware some additional exclusions apply to her stamps. For example, fading, creasing, denting, scratching, tearing, or thinning of her stamps is excluded.

Educational Objective 3

3-1. The insurer can use the Actual Cash Value Settlement endorsement (HO 04 81), which replaces the entire Loss Settlement condition with a statement that covered property losses will be settled at actual cash value at the time of loss, not to exceed the cost to repair or replace.

3-2. Using the Personal Property Replacement Cost Loss Settlement endorsement, an insurer will pay no more than the least of the following amounts: replacement cost at the time of loss without deduction for depreciation; full cost of repair; Coverage C limit; any applicable special limit; or the limit that applies to an item that is separately described and specifically insured.

3-3. Functional Replacement Cost Loss Settlement endorsement (HO 05 30) allows an insured to base building loss settlement on the cost to repair or replace using common materials and methods. Owners of old homes often prefer this approach over regular replacement cost loss settlement because the building limit can be set for a lower amount, thus reducing the policy premium to a more affordable level.

3-4. George can use the Personal Property Replacement Cost Loss Settlement endorsement (HO 04 90). This endorsement insures this type of property on a replacement cost basis instead of on an actual cash value basis.

Educational Objective 4

4-1. The insurer can decline or nonrenew coverage for the entire homeowners policy. Alternatively, the insurer can exclude personal and advertising injury liability coverage from the Home Business endorsement. This can be done using the Exclusion—Personal and Advertising Injury endorsement (HO 07 53).

4-2. Permitted Incidental Occupancies—Residence Premises endorsement (HO 04 42) extends the HO form to cover a permitted incidental occupancy in the dwelling or in an "other structure" on the residence premises. Permitted incidental occupancies include dance studios.

4-3. Home Day Care Coverage Endorsement (HO 04 97) extends the HO policy to cover property and liability exposures arising out of a home day care business being conducted at the residence premises.

4-4. The neighbor is likely referring to the Home Business Insurance Coverage endorsement (HO 07 01). To be eligible for this endorsement, the repair shop must be owned by the named insured, Bob, and residents of the named insured's household, which Dave is not. Even if the two friends solved that problem by making Dave a manager, rather than a co-owner, the coverage would be incomplete. Bob and Dave must still acquire additional policies to cover any auto, workers compensation, management liability, professional liability, cyber risk, crime, or other exposures not covered by the endorsed HO policy.

Educational Objective 5

5-1. Endorsement HO 05 41 is not needed when the insured is covered under an HO-5, or under an HO-4 or HO-6 that has been endorsed to provide open perils coverage.

5-2. Endorsement HO 17 33 modifies the Coverage C exclusion of property in an apartment regularly rented to others by an insured so that it does not apply to the residence premises.

5-3. In this situation, property insurance for the additional residence can be provided in a dwelling policy.

5-4. Yes, the Additional Residence Rented to Others 1, 2, 3 or 4 Families (HO 24 70) can be added to Samantha's HO policy to extend Section II—Liability Coverages to the rental properties.

Educational Objective 6

6-1. The Assisted Living Care Coverage endorsement (HO 04 59) extends Coverage C to include personal property owned and used by the person named in the schedule, subject to additional special limits for items such as hearing aids, eyeglasses, false teeth, and wheelchairs. The endorsement also adds these exclusions to Coverage E—Personal Liability: "liability assumed by the facility prior to an occurrence," and "bodily injury to a care facility professional or support staff that occurs while such person is on or off duty and attending to the person named in the Schedule."

6-2. The Watercraft endorsement (HO 24 75) can extend Section II—Liability Coverages to scheduled watercraft that exceed the 25 total horsepower requirement for watercraft coverage under the HO forms. However, in most cases, a separate boatowners policy will provide better liability damage coverage for boats than a homeowners policy can.

6-3. The Personal Injury Coverage endorsement (HO 24 82) extends Coverage E—Personal Liability of a homeowners policy to cover personal injury as defined in the endorsement. The endorsement defines personal injury to include one or more of the following offenses: false arrest, detention, or imprisonment; malicious prosecution, wrongful eviction, slander or libel; and violation of a person's right of privacy.

6-4. Without being endorsed, Harry's homeowners policy covers liability for use of a snowmobile on an insured location (with some exceptions). That does not include trails. However, he could add the Owned Snowmobile endorsement (HO 24 64), which extends Section II—Liability Coverages to cover the snowmobile owned by Harry and used off an insured location, such as on the trails.

Educational Objective 7

7-1. John and Cynthia should consider adding these endorsements:

a. To obtain open perils coverage (including broad coverage for breakage), John could purchase the Scheduled Personal Property Endorsement (HO 04 61). To obtain replacement cost coverage, instead of actual cash value coverage, on such property, John could purchase the Personal Property Replacement Cost Loss Settlement endorsement (HO 04 90), which would provide replacement cost coverage on most personal property covered under John and Cynthia's homeowners policy, including John's musical instruments.

b. Cynthia should consider adding the Home Business Insurance Coverage endorsement (HO 07 01). She also may wish to purchase coverage for spoilage of her flower inventory by adding the Special Coverage—Spoilage of Perishable Stock endorsement (HO 07 55).

c. John and Cynthia can extend their homeowners property and liability coverage to the garage apartment structure by purchasing the Structures Rented to Others endorsement (HO 04 40). They can cover the apartment furnishings to their full value by purchasing the Landlord's Furnishings endorsement (HO 05 46). Otherwise, they would have only $2,500 coverage for the furnishings.

Direct Your Learning 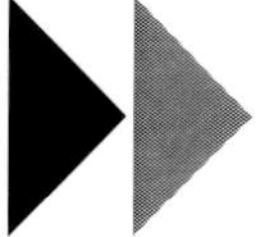

8

Other Residential Insurance Coverages

Educational Objectives

After learning the content of this assignment, you should be able to:

1. Contrast the Dwelling Property 3—Special Form (DP-3) policy with the Homeowners 3—Special Form policy in regard to each of the following:
   - Types of property covered
   - Other coverages
   - Perils insured against
   - Exclusions and conditions
   - Coverage for liability and theft losses
2. Given a case describing a dwelling claim, determine whether the Dwelling Property—Special Form (DP-3) policy would cover the claim and, if so, the amount the insurer would pay for the claim.
3. Summarize the coverages provided by personal inland marine policies.
4. Summarize the coverage provided by each of the following types of farm insurance coverages:
   - Insurance Services Office, Inc. (ISO) Farm Program
   - ISO Homeowners endorsements
   - Specialty farm and ranch programs
5. Describe the operation of FAIR plans and beachfront and windstorm plans and the coverage they provide.
6. Describe the operation of the National Flood Insurance Program and the coverage it provides.
7. Given a case describing a claim involving an individual or a family with a National Flood Insurance Policy, determine what is covered, excluded, or limited, and for what amounts.

Outline

- **Dwelling Policies**
  - A. Structures Eligible for Dwelling Policies
  - B. Coverages
  - C. Other Coverages
  - D. Perils Insured Against
  - E. Dwelling Policy General Exclusions
  - F. Dwelling Policy Conditions
  - G. Coverage for Liability and Theft Losses
- **Dwelling Coverage Case Study**
  - A. Case Facts
  - B. Case Analysis Tools
  - C. Determination of Coverage
  - D. Determination of Amounts Payable
- **Inland Marine Floaters**
  - A. Characteristics and Components
  - B. Common Policy Provisions
  - C. Coverages
    - 1. Personal Articles Standard Loss Settlement Form
    - 2. Personal Property Form
    - 3. Personal Effects Form
- **Farm Insurance Coverages**
  - A. ISO Farm Program
  - B. ISO Homeowners Endorsements
    - 1. Incidental Farming Personal Liability Endorsement
    - 2. Farmers Personal Liability Endorsement
  - C. Specialty Farm and Ranch Programs
- **FAIR and Beachfront and Windstorm Plans**
  - A. FAIR Plans
    - 1. Purpose and Operation
    - 2. Eligible Property
    - 3. Coverages
  - B. Beachfront and Windstorm Plans
    - 1. Purpose and Operation
    - 2. Eligible Property
    - 3. Coverages
- **The National Flood Insurance Program**
  - A. Community Eligibility
  - B. Incentives and Programs
    - 1. Emergency Program
    - 2. Regular Program
  - C. Flood Insurance Coverage
    - 1. Waiting Period
    - 2. Write-Your-Own (WYO) Program
  - D. Flood Insurance Reform
- **National Flood Insurance Program Coverage Case Study**
  - A. Case Facts
  - B. Case Analysis Tools
  - C. Determination of Coverage
  - D. Determination of Amounts Payable

Set aside a specific, realistic amount of time to study every day.

For each assignment, you should define or describe each of the Key Words and Phrases and answer each of the Review and Application Questions.

Educational Objective 1

Contrast the Dwelling Property 3—Special Form (DP-3) policy with the Homeowners 3—Special Form policy in regard to each of the following:

- **Types of property covered**
- **Other coverages**
- **Perils insured against**
- **Exclusions and conditions**
- **Coverage for liability and theft losses**

Review Questions

1-1. Describe what dwelling policies may be used for, other than insuring one- to four-family dwellings, whether owner-occupied or tenant-occupied.

1-2. Explain what coverage is provided by the Insurance Services Office, Inc. (ISO) Dwelling Property 3—Special Form (DP-3) form for increased costs the insured incurs because of the enforcement of any ordinance or law.

1-3. Explain how coverage for direct physical loss to real property is determined in both the DP-3 and Homeowners 3—Special Form (HO-3) forms.

1-4. Explain how the exclusions and additional coverages in the personal liability supplement attached to the ISO DP-3 compare to those applicable to Section II of the homeowners policy.

1-5. Describe the risk control measures that can be used to prevent or mitigate a theft of property not part of a covered structure.

Application Questions

1-6. If the insured owns a ladder that is kept along the fence in the backyard of the insured dwelling and uses it while cleaning the gutters at the insured location, would the ladder be included under Coverage A (if the insured did not purchase Coverage C—Personal Property)?

1-7. A house insured by a DP-3 was vacant for a month and then burglarized. The thief broke the framing of a door to get in and damaged several kitchen cabinet drawers while searching for valuables. What is covered?

Educational Objective 2

Given a case describing a dwelling claim, determine whether the Dwelling Property—Special Form (DP-3) policy would cover the claim and, if so, the amount the insurer would pay for the claim.

Application Questions

2-1. Scott and Sue have an Insurance Services Office, Inc. (ISO) Dwelling Property 3—Special Form (DP-3) policy on their home. The home is adjacent to a factory that emits smoke from its smokestacks. While Scott and Sue were away on vacation, they left an upstairs back window open. Atmospheric conditions caused the smoke from the factory to accumulate and linger rather than dissipate. The smoke entered the open window of Scott and Sue's home and damaged drapes and upholstered furniture. Does the couple's policy cover this loss?

2-2. Josh, a single father, owns a home where he lives with his two children, Lisa, age three, and Mia, age eleven. Josh has an ISO DP-3 policy on the home. On May 25, a fire caused extensive smoke damage to the interior of the house and its furnishings; Josh's DP-3 covered the damage. While the home was being repaired, Josh rented an apartment for his family to stay in for $1,200 a month. Because Mia was to spend the entire month of July at camp, Josh enrolled Lisa in a daycare center located near the apartment. Although the house became habitable July 15, Josh and Lisa remained in the apartment until Mia returned on August 1. Explain how Josh's insurer would handle their additional living expenses for that period.

2-3. A house insured by an ISO DP-3 policy was vacant for a month and then was burglarized. The thief broke the framing of a door to get in and damaged several kitchen cabinet drawers while searching for valuables. What is covered?

Educational Objective 3

Summarize the coverages provided by personal inland marine policies.

Key Words and Phrases

Inland marine insurance

Residence premises

Scheduled coverage

Blanket basis

Inherent vice

Personal effects

Review Questions

3-1. Explain why some insureds might need personal inland marine insurance.

3-2. Identify the general characteristics shared by personal inland marine policies.

3-3. Describe the types of coverage listed in the Conditions section of Insurance Services Office, Inc. (ISO) Common Policy Provisions of a personal inland marine policy.

3-4. How is the amount payable for a covered loss determined according to the Common Policy Conditions applying to scheduled coverage?

3-5. What are the two types of coverage forms available in the ISO personal inland marine program?

3-6. Describe the type of coverage provided by the Personal Property Form of the ISO personal inland marine program.

3-7. Explain why the Personal Effects Form of the ISO personal inland marine program is designed for frequent travelers.

Application Question

3-8. Larry sold his home and most of his furniture. He is spending at least two years traveling by bicycle across the United States and Europe. He is traveling with camera equipment valued at $8,000. He also placed some furniture, books, and personal possessions in a self-storage unit. What personal inland marine policies can Larry purchase to cover his property?

Educational Objective 4

Summarize the coverage provided by each of the following types of farm insurance coverages:

- **Insurance Services Office, Inc. (ISO) Farm Program**
- **ISO Homeowners endorsements**
- **Specialty farm and ranch programs**

Key Words and Phrases

Crop hail insurance

Animal mortality insurance

Feedlot insurance

Feedlot

Review Questions

4-1. The Insurance Services Office, Inc. (ISO) farm liability form combines what elements to provide adequate liability coverage for farms?

4-2. What intended operations does the Incidental Farming Personal Liability Endorsement cover?

4-3. What two specialty farm and ranch programs have been developed for farms and agribusinesses that involve livestock?

Educational Objective 5

Describe the operation of FAIR plans and beachfront and windstorm plans and the coverage they provide.

Key Words and Phrases

Syndicate

Difference in conditions (DIC) policy, or DIC insurance

Review Questions

5-1. What is the purpose of a Fair Access to Insurance Requirements (FAIR) plan (or a beachfront and windstorm plan)?

5-2. Describe three types of loss exposures that resulted in the creation of FAIR plans.

5-3. Explain how FAIR plans provide insurance, service policies, and fund losses paid under the plan.

5-4. If a FAIR plan administrator finds that a property fails to meet the basic safety levels, can the owner obtain coverage under a state FAIR plan? Explain your answer.

5-5. What four coverages are usually available under FAIR plans?

5-6. Describe the various operations of beachfront and windstorm plans.

5-7. What requirements do states have for properties to be eligible for coverage under beachfront and windstorm plans?

5-8. What are the two primary perils insured against under beachfront and windstorm plans?

5-9. What special provision under beachfront and windstorm plans might restrict applications for new coverage and/or increases in limits?

Application Question

5-10. Sarah wishes to purchase an expensive home in a suburb that is located near a heavily wooded area. Because of the increased fire hazard, she is unable to obtain insurance for the property. The financing organization requires insurance coverage and recommends that Sarah apply for coverage under the state FAIR plan.

a. What must Sarah do for her otherwise uninsurable property to be eligible under the FAIR plan?

b. Because Sarah's state FAIR plan provides only fire, vandalism, riot, and windstorm coverages, and the financing organization requires coverage against all common homeowners perils, what action should Sarah take to obtain the needed coverage? Explain your answer.

Educational Objective 6

Describe the operation of the National Flood Insurance Program and the coverage it provides.

Key Words and Phrases

Special flood hazard area (SFHA)

Flood hazard boundary map

Emergency program

Flood Insurance Rate Map (FIRM)

Regular program

Write-Your-Own (WYO) program

Review Questions

6-1. Describe the two ways a community's residents become eligible for flood insurance under the National Flood Insurance Program (NFIP).

6-2. Describe the assistance available to special flood hazard area (SFHA) residents not participating in the NFIP if disaster occurs as a result of flooding in a community, and any special restrictions on assistance.

6-3. Describe the insurance that property owners can purchase when a community first joins the NFIP and the actions the FIA takes when a community first joins the NFIP.

6-4. Describe the three federal flood insurance policies available to insureds.

6-5. How long is the waiting period required by the NFIP, and why is it required?

6-6. Describe the exception to the NFIP's waiting period.

6-7. Describe the roles of the FIA, NFIP, and an insurer participating in the Write-Your-Own (WYO) program.

Application Question

6-8. Karen purchased a home for $250,000 in a community that is eligible for flood insurance under the NFIP emergency program. Karen's home is in a special flood hazard area. What incentive does Karen have to encourage her community to enter the NFIP regular program as soon as possible?

Educational Objective 7

Given a case describing a claim involving an individual or a family with a National Flood Insurance Policy, determine what is covered, excluded, or limited, and for what amounts.

Application Question

7-1. Louis and Pearl live in a one-story single-family dwelling located in a flood-prone area. The home is valued at $125,000, and the contents are valued at $40,000. The community in which this dwelling is located is currently eligible under the National Flood Insurance Program's (NFIP's) emergency program. Louis notices in his local newspaper that the community will soon be eligible under NFIP's regular program.

a. What amounts of coverage are available for this dwelling under the emergency program?

b. If the community qualifies for the regular program, will additional coverage be available for this dwelling?

Answers to Assignment 8 Questions

NOTE: These answers are provided to give students a basic understanding of acceptable types of responses. They often are not the only valid answers and are not intended to provide an exhaustive response to the questions.

Educational Objective 1

1-1. Dwelling policies may also be used for other kinds of property and activities:

- A dwelling in the course of construction
- Mobile homes at a permanent location
- Houseboats, in some states
- Certain incidental business occupancies, if the businesses are operated by the owner-insured or by a tenant of the insured location

1-2. If the insured has purchased Coverage A, ordinance or law coverage is provided up to 10 percent of the Coverage A limit. If there is no Coverage A limit, up to 10 percent of the Coverage B limit is provided for ordinance or law coverage. This coverage is additional insurance.

1-3. In both the DP-3 and the HO-3 forms, the coverage for direct physical loss to real property is determined by the causes of loss that are excluded. Those causes of loss that are not excluded are covered.

1-4. The exclusions and additional coverages in the personal liability supplement attached to the DP-3 are virtually the same as those applicable to Section II of the homeowners policy. The main difference is that the additional liability coverage for loss assessment provided (up to a limit of $1,000) in the HO-3 form is not provided in the personal liability supplement.

1-5. Appropriate risk control measures include these:

- Lock all doors and windows
- Install a security system
- Store valuables in a safety deposit box at a bank

1-6. Yes, the dwelling form specifically states that, if not covered elsewhere in the policy, building equipment and outdoor equipment used for the service of the premises and located on the described location are covered.

1-7. Theft of personal property is not covered under the DP-3, but coverage is provided for damage to covered property caused by burglars, unless the dwelling has been vacant for more than sixty days. Since the house was vacant for only a month the policy still provides some coverage. The damage to both the door frame and the drawers is covered. Whatever items of value found in the drawers that were stolen by the thief would not be covered.

Educational Objective 2

2-1. The damage to Scott and Sue's furniture would not be covered under their DP-3 because smoke from agricultural smudging or industrial operations is excluded in Coverage C—Personal Property.

2-2. The insurer would cover the family's additional living expenses only until July 15, when their home became habitable. Josh would be responsible for the family's additional living expenses after July 15.

2-3. Theft of personal property is not covered under the DP-3, but coverage is provided for damage to covered property caused by burglars, unless the dwelling has been vacant for more than sixty days. Because the house was vacant for only a month, the policy still provides some coverage. The damage to both the door frame and the drawers is covered. Any items of value found in the drawers that were stolen by the thief would not be covered.

Educational Objective 3

3-1. Some insureds might need personal inland marine insurance because of the restrictive nature of some personal property coverages under a homeowners policy. Personal inland marine policies can provide higher limits of insurance for losses of a particular type or that occur at a particular location.

3-2. Personal inland marine policies share these general characteristics:

- The coverage is tailored to the specific type of property to be insured, such as jewelry, cameras, or musical instruments.
- The insured may select the appropriate policy limits.
- Policies are often written without a deductible.
- Most policies insure property worldwide with special form coverage (open perils), subject to exclusions.

3-3. The Conditions section of the Common Policy Provisions specifies that insured property may have scheduled coverage by which articles or items are specifically listed. The Conditions section also specifies that insured property may have unscheduled coverage by which articles are covered on a blanket basis, such as stamps or coins in a collection.

3-4. With certain exceptions, the amount paid for a covered loss is the least of four amounts:

- The actual cash value of the insured property at the time of loss or damage
- The amount for which the insured could reasonably be expected to have the property repaired to its condition immediately before loss
- The amount for which the insured could reasonably be expected to replace the property with property substantially identical to the lost or damaged article
- The amount of insurance stated in the policy

3-5. In the ISO personal inland marine program, two types of coverage forms are available:

- Specialized forms are used to cover a single category of personal property, such as outboard motors and boats, fine arts, cameras, or motorized golf carts.
- General forms are broader and generic in nature. These three general forms (Personal Articles Standard Loss Settlement Form, Personal Property Form, and Personal Effects Form) are commonly used to provide coverage on a single form for many kinds of personal property.

3-6. The Personal Property Form provides special form coverage on unscheduled personal property owned or used by the insured and normally kept at the insured's residence. The form also provides worldwide coverage on the same property when it is temporarily away from the residence premises. The Personal Property Form can be used to insure thirteen classes of unscheduled personal property, such as silverware, cameras, and major appliances.

3-7. The Personal Effects Form is designed for frequent travelers because it provides special form coverage on personal property such as luggage, clothes, cameras, and sports equipment normally worn or carried by tourists and travelers. The form covers property worldwide, but only while the property is away from the insured's permanent residence.

3-8. A Personal Effects Form can be used to cover the camera equipment. The Personal Property Form can be used to insure the property in the self-storage unit.

Educational Objective 4

4-1. The ISO farm liability form combines elements of homeowners liability coverage and commercial general liability coverage, and it includes special provisions to address liability loss exposures unique to farms.

4-2. The Incidental Farming Personal Liability Endorsement is intended to cover farming or garden operations that are not the insured's principal occupation.

4-3. Animal mortality insurance and feedlot insurance are specialty farm and ranch programs that have been developed for farms and agribusinesses that involve livestock.

Educational Objective 5

5-1. A FAIR plan (or a beachfront and windstorm plan) makes property insurance coverage available when insurers in the voluntary market cannot profitably provide coverage at a rate that is reasonable for policyholders and provide the needed support for credit.

5-2. FAIR plans were created to respond to three types of losses:

- Riot and civil commotion in urban areas
- Windstorm damage to coastal properties
- Brush fires in some wooded, suburban areas

5-3. Whether the FAIR plan operates as a policy-issuing syndicate or contracts with one or more voluntary insurers to act as servicing organizations for a percentage of premiums, the organizations perform underwriting, policyholder service, and claim handling functions. In most FAIR plans, all licensed property insurers are required to share payment for plan losses in proportion to their share of property insurance premiums collected.

5-4. If a property fails to meet the basic safety levels, the owner can be required to make improvements as a condition for obtaining insurance under the FAIR plan. If the problems are not corrected, the state can deny insurance, provided the exposures are not related to the neighborhood location or to hazardous environmental conditions beyond the owner's control.

5-5. FAIR plans usually cover fire, vandalism, riot, and windstorm.

5-6. Some states offer beachfront and windstorm plans that operate using a single servicing organization that provides the underwriting, policyholders services, and claim handling services. Others operate as policy-issuing syndicates in which the plan issues the policies and the plan's staff provides services. In all plans, insurers that write property coverages in that state are required to share in plan losses in proportion to their share of state property insurance premiums.

5-7. Properties eligible for coverage under beachfront and windstorm plans must be ineligible for coverage in the voluntary market and must be located in designated coastal areas. In some states they must be located within a certain distance of the shoreline. Each plan requires that buildings constructed or rebuilt after a specified date conform to an applicable building code.

5-8. The two primary perils insured against under beachfront and windstorm plans are wind and hail.

5-9. Under beachfront and windstorm plans, when a hurricane has formed within a certain distance of the beach area where the property is located, special provisions might restrict applications for new coverage and/or increases in limits.

5-10. These answers address questions regarding Sarah's state FAIR plan:

a. Sarah must have the property inspected by the state FAIR plan administrator. The property must meet FAIR plan inspection criteria, which include basic safety levels, or she must make any recommended improvements to the property before it will be eligible.

b. Because Sarah's state FAIR plan provides coverage against limited perils, Sarah should apply for a difference in conditions policy (DIC) through a specialty insurer. This policy excludes direct loss caused by fire and the other perils covered under the FAIR plan, but it covers the other common homeowners perils.

Educational Objective 6

6-1. A community's residents become eligible for flood insurance under the NFIP in two ways:

a. The community applies to the Federal Insurance Administration (FIA) to be included in the NFIP.

b. The Federal Emergency Management Agency (FEMA) determines that an area is flood-prone and notifies the community that it has one year to decide whether to join the NFIP. A community that chooses not to join the NFIP is not eligible for federal flood assistance.

6-2. If a disaster occurs as a result of flooding in a nonparticipating community, no federal financial assistance can be provided for the permanent repair or reconstruction of insurable buildings in SFHAs. Eligible applicants for disaster assistance may, however, receive forms of disaster assistance that are not related to permanent repair and reconstruction of buildings. If a community is accepted into the NFIP within six months of a disaster, these limitations on federal disaster assistance are lifted.

6-3. When a community first joins the NFIP, property owners in special flood hazard areas can purchase limited amounts of insurance at subsidized rates under the initial phase of the program, called the emergency program. Although the community is eligible under the emergency program, the FIA arranges for a detailed study of the community and its susceptibility to flood. The study results in the publication of a Flood Insurance Rate Map (FIRM) that divides the community into specific zones to identify the probability of flooding in each zone.

6-4. Three federal flood insurance policies are available to insureds:

a. The dwelling form is used for any dwelling having an occupancy of no more than four families, such as single-family homes, townhouses, row houses, and individual condominium units.

b. The general property form is used for all other occupancies—that is, multi-residential and nonresidential, except for residential condominium building associations.

c. Residential condominium building associations are eligible for coverage under the residential condominium building association form.

6-5. The NFIP generally requires a thirty-day waiting period for new flood insurance policies and for endorsements that increase coverage on existing policies. The waiting period prevents adverse selection.

6-6. An exception to the NFIP's waiting period is made for flood insurance that is purchased initially in connection with a property purchase or a new or an increased mortgage on a property. In such cases, the policy becomes effective at the time the property is transferred or the mortgage becomes effective, provided that the policy is applied for and the premium paid at or before the transfer of ownership or date of mortgage.

6-7. In the WYO program, the FIA determines rates, coverage limitations, and eligibility. Insurers collect premiums, retain commissions, and use the remainder of the premiums to pay claims. Insurers receive an expense allowance for policies written and claims processed, while the federal government retains responsibility for losses. The NFIP totally reinsures the coverage.

6-8. While the community is in the emergency flood insurance program, only $35,000 in flood insurance is available. If the community complies with the flood control and land-use restrictions required by the NFIP, and the maps are created for the specific flood zones, the community may change to the regular flood program. Under the regular flood program, up to $250,000 coverage is available for dwellings.

Educational Objective 7

7-1. These answers apply to the NFIP case:

a. The maximum limits available for a single-family dwelling are $35,000 for the dwelling and $10,000 for the contents. Louis and Pearl could only insure the home and its contents for these amounts.

b. Yes, once the community is eligible for NFIP's regular program, the maximum limits for a single-family dwelling increase to $250,000 on the dwelling and $100,000 for the contents. Louis and Pearl could then apply for full coverage of $125,000 for the dwelling and $40,000 for the contents.

Direct Your Learning

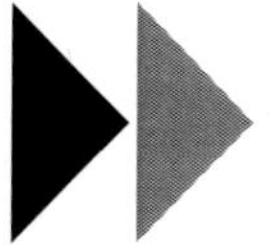

9

Watercraft, RVs, Mobile Homes, and Excess Liability

Educational Objectives

After learning the content of this assignment, you should be able to:

1. Explain how individuals and families can use insurance to treat loss exposures related to the following miscellaneous vehicles:
   - Motor homes and recreational trailers
   - Motorcycles and other two-wheeled vehicles
   - Snowmobiles
   - Golf carts
   - Antique and classic automobiles
   - Other recreational vehicles
2. Explain what loss exposures are covered and what is limited or excluded by the following types of mobile home coverages:
   - The Insurance Services Office, Inc. (ISO) Mobilehome Endorsement
   - Other ISO mobilehome endorsements
   - Specialty insurers' mobile home policies
3. Explain how individuals and families can treat their watercraft loss exposures using each of the following:
   - Small boat policies
   - Boatowners and yacht policies
   - Insurance Services Office, Inc. (ISO) Personal Lines Watercraft Policy Program
   - ISO Homeowners Coverage Forms
   - Personal Auto Policy

9

Educational Objectives, continued

4. Summarize the coverage provided by the typical personal umbrella policy.
5. Given a case describing a liability claim, determine the following:
   - Whether the loss would be covered by a personal umbrella policy
   - The dollar amount, if any, payable under the umbrella policy
   - The dollar amount, if any, payable under the underlying insurance policies
   - The dollar amount, if any, payable by the insured

Outline

- **Coverage for Miscellaneous Vehicles**
    - A. Motor Homes and Recreational Trailers
    - B. Motorcycles and Other Two-Wheeled Vehicles
    - C. Snowmobiles
    - D. Golf Carts
    - E. Antique and Classic Automobiles
    - F. Other Recreational Vehicles
- **Mobile Home Insurance**
    - A. The ISO Mobilehome Endorsement
    - B. Other ISO Mobilehome Endorsements
    - C. Specialty Insurers' Mobilehome Policies
- **Personal Watercraft Insurance**
    - A. Small Boat Policies
    - B. Boatowners and Yacht Policies
    - C. ISO Personal Lines Watercraft Policy Program
    - D. ISO Homeowners Coverage Forms
    - E. Personal Auto Policy
- **Personal Umbrella Liability Insurance**
    - A. Purposes of Personal Umbrella Coverage
    - B. Personal Umbrella Coverages
        - 1. Insuring Agreement
        - 2. Exclusions
        - 3. Conditions
- **Umbrella Coverage Case Study**
    - A. Case Facts
    - B. Case Analysis Tools
    - C. Determination of Coverage
        - 1. Auto Accident
        - 2. Slander Lawsuit
    - D. Determination of Amounts Payable

Writing notes as you read your materials will help you remember key pieces of information.

For each assignment, you should define or describe each of the Key Words and Phrases and answer each of the Review and Application Questions.

Educational Objective 1

Explain how individuals and families can use insurance to treat loss exposures related to the following miscellaneous vehicles:

- **Motor homes and recreational trailers**
- **Motorcycles and other two-wheeled vehicles**
- **Snowmobiles**
- **Golf carts**
- **Antique and classic automobiles**
- **Other recreational vehicles**

Key Words and Phrases

Miscellaneous type vehicles

Lay-up provision

Vicarious liability

Review Questions

1-1. Describe risk finance techniques for liability and property loss exposures resulting from golf cart ownership.

1-2. Describe two coverage features common in specialty policies for motor homes.

1-3. Contrast two ways insurers may apply a passenger hazards exclusion in a Snowmobile Endorsement to the Personal Auto Policy (PAP.)

Educational Objective 2

Explain what loss exposures are covered and what is limited or excluded by the following types of mobile home coverages:

- **The Insurance Services Office, Inc. (ISO) Mobilehome Endorsement**
- **Other ISO mobilehome endorsements**
- **Specialty insurers' mobile home policies**

Key Words and Phrases

Mobilehome Endorsement

Ordinance or Law Coverage endorsement

Review Questions

2-1. Describe the purpose of the Mobilehome Endorsement.

2-2. Explain why the limit for Coverage C—Personal Property is usually lower on Insurance Services Office, Inc. (ISO) mobilehome policies than it is on homeowners policies.

2-3. Describe the coverage provided by the Mobilehome Lienholder's Single Interest Endorsement.

Educational Objective 3

Explain how individuals and families can treat their watercraft loss exposures using each of the following:

- **Small boat policies**
- **Boatowners and yacht policies**
- **Insurance Services Office, Inc. (ISO) Personal Lines Watercraft Policy Program**
- **ISO Homeowners Coverage Forms**
- **Personal Auto Policy**

Key Words and Phrases

Perils of the sea

Warranty

Hull insurance

Protection and indemnity (P&I) insurance

Jones Act (United States Merchant Marine Act of 1920)

Review Questions

3-1. Describe two options to provide liability insurance for a 32-foot sailboat.

3-2. Contrast the insurance coverage for property damage to a small boat under an Insurance Services Office, Inc. (ISO) Homeowners 3—Special Form (HO-3) policy with the coverage under an ISO Watercraft Program policy.

3-3. Provide two examples of typical warranties in boatowners and yacht insurance policies.

Educational Objective 4

Summarize the coverage provided by the typical personal umbrella policy.

Review Questions

4-1. Joe is considering purchasing a personal umbrella policy. Who would be covered under this policy?

4-2. Explain how drop-down coverage applies to a personal umbrella policy.

4-3. Briefly describe the most important conditions in the personal umbrella policy.

Application Question

4-4. Explain whether each of the following losses would be covered by a typical personal umbrella policy.

a. Until the police arrived, the insured detained a youth falsely accused of stealing a racing bike. The police later arrested the actual thief. The youth's parents sued the insured for the false arrest of their son.

b. The insured owns a small bakery and is sued when an employee severely burns his hand when an oven's handle falls off.

Educational Objective 5

Given a case describing a liability claim, determine the following:

- **Whether the loss would be covered by a personal umbrella policy**
- **The dollar amount, if any, payable under the umbrella policy**
- **The dollar amount, if any, payable under the underlying insurance policies**
- **The dollar amount, if any, payable by the insured**

Review Question

5-1. Eileen and Robert are a married couple who own a home and two vehicles for which they are the only drivers. The Insurance Services Office, Inc. (ISO) Homeowners 3—Special Form (HO-3) policy includes liability coverage with a $500,000 per occurrence limit. The vehicles are insured under a personal auto policy (PAP) with split limits of $250,000 per person/ $500,000 per occurrence. The couple also carry a personal umbrella policy with a $1 million limit, a $500,000 deductible (retained limit), and a $1,000 self-insured retention (SIR). All policies list Eileen and Robert as named insureds.

Robert is in an auto accident involving a collision with two other vehicles and is found liable for injuries to the other two drivers. The first claimant was awarded $282,000 for bodily injury, and the second claimant was awarded $325,000 for bodily injury.

a. What amounts, if any, will be paid under the PAP and under the personal umbrella policy?

b. Eileen and Robert fail to pay the premium for their auto policy, and the coverage is canceled. Payments were made on the HO-3 and the personal umbrella policies to keep them in force. What amounts would be paid for Robert's auto accident in this instance?

Answers to Assignment 9 Questions

NOTE: These answers are provided to give students a basic understanding of acceptable types of responses. They often are not the only valid answers and are not intended to provide an exhaustive response to the questions.

Educational Objective 1

1-1. Liability coverage for golf carts is available under Insurance Services Office, Inc. (ISO) homeowners policies, the Miscellaneous Type Vehicle Endorsement to the PAP, or a specialty policy. Property coverage for golf carts is available with the Owned Motorized Golf Cart Physical Loss Coverage Endorsement to the homeowners policy, the Miscellaneous Type Vehicle Endorsement to the PAP, or a specialty policy.

1-2. Common features in specialty policies for motor homes include coverage for personal property and household furnishings lost or damaged by a covered peril, vacation expense coverage for expenses such as a motel room if the motor home becomes uninhabitable as a result of a covered peril while the insured is on vacation, or a lay-up provision that reduces premium for a portion of the year when the motor home is not in use.

1-3. Some insurers may require a passenger hazards exclusion, while other insurers may offer a passenger hazards exclusion as an option to reduce premium.

Educational Objective 2

2-1. The Mobilehome Endorsement is a homeowners endorsement form that broadens HO-2 or HO-3 coverage to include common mobilehome exposures.

2-2. The limit for Coverage C—Personal Property is usually lower because many of the built-in accessories and furniture in the mobile home are covered as part of the dwelling.

2-3. This endorsement provides coverage only to the lienholder for transportation exposures or any loss from the owner's embezzlement of the mobile home.

Educational Objective 3

3-1. The sailboat could be insured with either a yacht policy or an Insurance Services Office, Inc. (ISO) Watercraft Program policy.

3-2. The HO-3 limits coverage, while an ISO Watercraft Program policy provides broader coverage.

3-3. Examples of warranties in typical boatowners and yacht insurance policies include any two of these four:

- The insured warrants that the boat will be used only for private, pleasure purposes and will not be hired or chartered unless the insurer approves.
- The insured warrants that the boat is in seaworthy condition.
- The insured warrants that the boat will not be in operation during any lay-up period.
- The insured warrants that the vessel will not be operated outside of the navigational limits stated in the declarations.

Educational Objective 4

4-1. The policy covers the named insured, resident relatives, and usually persons using (with the insured's permission) cars, motorcycles, recreational vehicles, or watercraft owned by or rented to the named insured. Also, persons younger than twenty-one who are in the care of the named insured or of a resident relative generally are covered.

4-2. The personal umbrella policy typically provides drop-down coverage, which is broader than the underlying coverage. When the underlying insurance does not apply to a particular loss and the loss is not excluded by the umbrella coverage, the umbrella coverage "drops down" to cover the entire loss, less a self-insured retention (SIR). Usually the retention is $250, but it can be as high as $10,000. The SIR applies only when the loss is not covered by an existing underlying policy.

4-3. These are among the most important conditions in the personal umbrella policy:

- The insured must maintain the underlying insurance coverages and limits shown in the declarations. If underlying coverage is not maintained, the policy will pay no more than would have been covered if the underlying insurance was in effect.
- The insured must give the insurer written notice of loss as soon as practicable.
- The umbrella policy is excess over any other insurance, whether collectible or not.
- The policy territory is worldwide.

4-4. These answers address questions regarding a typical personal umbrella policy:

a. Yes. The personal umbrella policy would cover the insured's liability for personal injury, including false arrest.

b. No. The personal umbrella policy would not cover any obligation for which the insured is legally liable under a workers compensation, disability benefits, or similar law.

Educational Objective 5

5-1. These answers address Eileen and Robert's case:

a. The PAP policy will pay $500,000 (the $250,000 per person limit for each claimant). The loss amount exceeds the $500,000 deductible on the personal umbrella policy, so that policy will also apply to this accident. The personal umbrella policy will pay $107,000 (the remaining $32,000 for the first claimant and the remaining $75,000 for the second claimant). Because the loss is covered by an underlying policy, the $1,000 SIR will not apply.

b. If underlying limits are not maintained, the umbrella policy will pay no more than would have been covered if the underlying insurance were in effect. The canceled PAP pays nothing. Because the loss amount exceeds the umbrella deductible, the personal umbrella liability policy will respond. The $500,000 deductible shown on the umbrella declarations page will be applied. The umbrella policy will pay $107,000 for this occurrence. Robert is responsible for the remaining $500,000.

Direct Your Learning

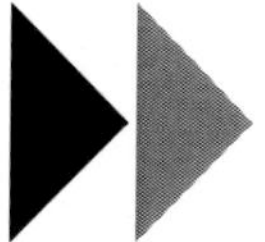

10

Personal Lines Profitability and Pricing

Educational Objectives

After learning the content of this assignment, you should be able to:

1. Explain how factors affect personal lines profitability goals for a portfolio and their effect on portfolio management.
2. Evaluate the effectiveness of methods for increasing personal lines profitability.
3. Explain how pricing components and relativity factors affect personal insurance profitability.
4. Explain how insurers analyze loss data and forecast trends.
5. Summarize factors that insurers apply to the ratemaking process, including regulatory objectives, social objectives, and investment income.
6. Given a case study regarding a personal lines portfolio that requires a rate adjustment to restore profitability, explain how a premium and loss analysis is performed, rate relativities are determined, and the adjustment of the base rate is applied.

Outline

- **Personal Lines Profitability Goals**
  - A. Planning and Goal Setting
  - B. Industry Trends
    1. How Industry Trends Affect Goals
    2. How Industry Trends Affect Portfolio Management
  - C. Individual Company Trends
    1. How Company Trends Affect Goals
    2. How Company Trends Affect Portfolio Management
  - D. Competition
    1. How Competition Affects Goals
    2. How Competition Affects Portfolio Management
  - E. Regulatory Changes
    1. How Regulatory Changes Affect Goals
    2. How Regulatory Changes Affect Portfolio Management
  - F. New and Retiring Product Lines
    1. How Changing Earned Premiums Affects Goals
    2. How Changing Earned Premiums Affects Portfolio Management
- **Increasing Personal Lines Profitability**
  - A. Increasing Premium
    1. Selective Growth
    2. Growth in Niche Markets
    3. Point-of-Sale Marketing
    4. Adjusting Rates and Relativity Factors
    5. Ease-of-Use Technology
    6. Improving Producer/Underwriter Relationships
  - B. Decreasing Losses
    1. Responding to Poor Loss Experience
    2. Checking Compliance With Underwriting Guidelines
    3. Adjusting Underwriting Guidelines
    4. Managing Catastrophe Exposures
    5. Reunderwriting
  - C. Controlling Expenses
    1. Maximizing Human Resources
    2. Managing Underwriting Expenses
    3. Outsourcing Underwriting Activities
- **Personal Lines Pricing**
  - A. Pure Premiums and Base Rates
  - B. Class Relativity Factors
    1. Residential Property Rate Relativities
    2. Personal Auto Rate Relativity Factors
- **Analyzing Loss Data and Forecasting Trends**
  - A. Loss Frequency Trends
  - B. Loss Severity Trends
  - C. Comparing Loss Frequency and Loss Severity Among Groups
    1. Frequency Analysis
    2. Severity Analysis
- **Ratemaking Principles**
  - A. Regulatory Objectives
    1. Not Inadequate
    2. Not Excessive
    3. Not Unfairly Discriminatory
  - B. Social Objectives
    1. Affordable
    2. Available
    3. Provide Risk Control Incentives
    4. Responsive to Change
    5. Provide Rate Stability
    6. Responsive to Controllable Rating Factors
  - C. Interest Income Considerations
- **Rate Adjustment Case Study**
  - A. Case Facts
  - B. Case Analysis Tools
  - C. Premium and Loss Analysis
    1. Calculating Loss Costs
    2. Comparing the Loss Costs of the Insurer With Industry Data
    3. Analyzing Frequency and Severity of Losses
    4. Checking to See Whether Losses Were Skewed by Events
  - D. Application of Rate Relativities
    1. Estimating What the Base Rate Should Have Been

Studying before sleeping helps you retain material better than studying before undertaking other tasks.

Outline

2. Developing Rate Relativity Factors From Projected Frequency and Severity
3. Applying Rate Relativity Factors to the Adequate Base Rate
4. Applying the Adjusted Base Rate

For each assignment, you should define or describe each of the Key Words and Phrases and answer each of the Review and Application Questions.

Educational Objective 1

Explain how factors affect personal lines profitability goals for a portfolio and their effect on portfolio management.

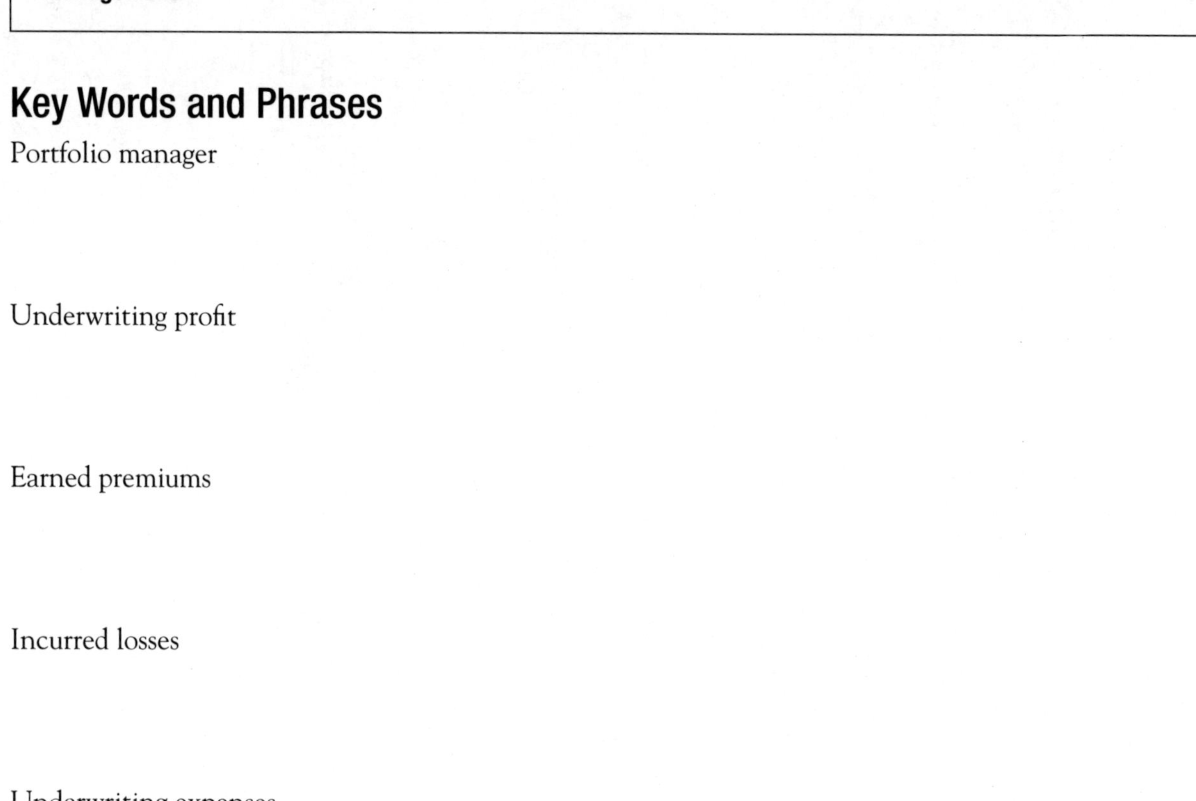

Key Words and Phrases

Portfolio manager

Underwriting profit

Earned premiums

Incurred losses

Underwriting expenses

Review Questions

1-1. Define underwriting profit, and describe how portfolio managers manage it.

1-2. Describe how each of the following affect portfolio management:

a. Company trends

b. Industry trends

c. Competition

d. Changes in earned premiums

Application Question

1-3. Southern Insurance's personal portfolio manager has learned that a competitor has introduced a new interface system in independent agents' offices. The computer interface offers an extremely easy-to-use quoting and entry system for homeowners and personal auto applications. Describe two changes that Southern Insurance's personal portfolio manager can expect as a result of this change by the competitor.

Educational Objective 2

Evaluate the effectiveness of methods for increasing personal lines profitability.

Key Word or Phrase

Reunderwriting

Review Questions

2-1. Describe three methods to mitigate or manage catastrophe exposures.

2-2. Insurers often respond to poor underwriting results by introducing expense control measures. Describe the three major ways insurers can control expenses.

Application Question

2-3. Alpha Insurance is a conservative company with historically restrictive underwriting guidelines that writes homeowners policies in the northeast region of the United States. Alpha has failed to meet its homeowners premium goals for the last year. The portfolio manager has been asked to evaluate the following two possible methods for increasing premium growth:

Educational Objective 3

Explain how pricing components and relativity factors affect personal insurance profitability.

Key Words and Phrases

Pure premium

Exposure unit

Factor out

Base rate

Base premiums

Loss development

Loss costs

Risk classification

Rate relativity factor

Unity classification

Review Questions

3-1. Describe the three-step process insurers use to adjust pricing to the different levels of risk within a portfolio.

3-2. Explain why it is necessary to modify the base rate for an insurance class or product with relativity factors, and give an example.

Application Question

3-3. A portfolio manager has recognized that homes within a portfolio with roofs over ten years old and roofs over fifteen years old have increasingly higher damage severity during windstorms. This is particularly apparent in windstorm-prone areas. Assuming that changing the company's underwriting guidelines is not an option, describe two recommendations the portfolio manager can make to ensure that adequate premium is charged for the roof loss exposures?

Educational Objective 4

Explain how insurers analyze loss data and forecast trends.

Key Words and Phrases

Loss frequency

Loss severity

Reserve takedown

Review Questions

4-1. Explain how actuaries typically express loss frequencies and identify loss frequency trends.

4-2. Describe loss severity trends.

4-3. Actuaries may exclude the effect of reserve takedowns from their loss severity calculations. Explain why they would exclude them.

4-4. Explain why actuaries compare and analyze the frequency and severity of losses among different groups.

▶▶

Educational Objective 5

Summarize factors that insurers apply to the ratemaking process, including regulatory objectives, social objectives, and investment Income.

Key Words and Phrases

Investment income

Realized capital gain

Unrealized capital gain

Review Questions

5-1. List the three regulatory objectives insurance rates must meet in all states.

5-2. Explain why actuaries should use caution when evaluating statewide insurance rate information to determine rate adequacy.

5-3. Indicate three ways that regulatory authorities may ensure that insurance rates are not excessive.

5-4. List the six social objectives insurers' rates must meet.

5-5. List the three sources insurers derive investment profit from.

Educational Objective 6

Given a case study regarding a personal lines portfolio that requires a rate adjustment to restore profitability, explain how a premium and loss analysis is performed, rate relativities are determined, and the adjustment of the base rate is applied.

Application Question

6-1. A medium-sized personal lines insurer is adjusting the pricing for its homeowners book of business within one state. The loss ratio within this territory has increased for each of the last five years and is currently 67 percent. The territory manager has requested an analysis of these results to determine whether a rate adjustment is needed.

a. Explain how the actuarial staff would calculate average loss costs for this book of business.

b. For the most current year, the loss costs for this book of business were $253. Pooled industry data for the same territory indicate loss costs of $352. Calculate the relative performance of this book, and describe the importance of these results to the actuaries.

c. The insurer's loss severity for the current year is 12 percent and was 9 percent in the prior year. Explain how the actuaries will develop rate relativity factors from projected severity.

Answers to Assignment 10 Questions

NOTE: These answers are provided to give students a basic understanding of acceptable types of responses. They often are not the only valid answers and are not intended to provide an exhaustive response to the questions.

Educational Objective 1

1-1. Underwriting profit is the income an insurer earns from premiums paid by policyholders minus incurred losses and underwriting expenses. Portfolio managers manage underwriting profit by measuring components of underwriting profit, monitoring changes in the components, comparing changes with goals, and then taking action to control the components.

1-2. These answers apply to questions regarding portfolio management:

a. Company trends generally affect portfolio management through small shifts in pricing or underwriting guidelines that affect written premium and losses. Exceptions occur when a company must make drastic changes to respond to a threat or an opportunity.

b. Portfolio managers need to monitor industry trends closely and recommend changes to respond, such as incremental premium increases or gradual changes in written premium goals.

c. Competition usually affects a portfolio's written premium; however, it can also negatively affect the loss ratio if there is adverse selection.

d. Changes in earned premiums for new and retiring product lines can result in exaggerated loss ratios and require continual monitoring.

1-3. Southern Insurance might expect a reduction in written premiums. If the reduction is significant enough, Southern might experience reduced earned premium and adverse selection, if the competitor has stricter underwriting guidelines.

Educational Objective 2

2-1. Insurers use various methods to mitigate or manage catastrophe exposures. (Any three of the following seven are acceptable.)

- Introducing policy exclusions and sublimits for loss exposures such as windstorm and earthquake
- Using reinsurance to limit the effect of catastrophe losses
- Joining risk-sharing pools with other insurers
- Increasing deductibles or introducing deductibles that are a percentage of the insured loss
- Offering lower deductibles and premium discounts to policyholders who make improvements according to safety or construction criteria
- Offsetting anticipated catastrophe losses by increasing lower-risk premium income from areas not as prone to catastrophes
- Monitoring the geographic redistribution of insured risks and limiting as much as possible the concentration of policies in areas prone to catastrophe

2-2. Insurers can use these methods to control expenses:

- Maximizing human resources through training employees to improve productivity and accuracy, using technology to improve efficiency, and providing appropriate incentives to attract and retain good employees.
- Managing underwriting expenses. Fixed underwriting expenses can be managed by consolidation of offices and job functions, increased efficiency through technology, increased focus on employees' expenses, and outsourcing of services. Variable expenses can be managed by decreasing commission rates or by increasing direct sales to consumers.
- Outsourcing underwriting activities such as application data verification services.

2-3. If Alpha is underinsuring homeowners policies, increasing coverage to the appropriate value is a conservative action to increase premiums. There is some expense involved in hiring a third-party vendor to conduct the assessments. However, a sample of policies could be performed to determine the effectiveness of the activity in increasing premiums in excess of the expenses required.

Home business would be a new niche market for Alpha. There is some risk in establishing appropriate underwriting guidelines and pricing the policies effectively. Also, the strength of the competition would have to be determined. The customer response to the new product is unknown, and it might be difficult to withdraw from the market, once initiated. If the volume of policies written is low, loss frequency and severity will be less predictable.

Considering the conservative nature of the company, the replacement cost assessment would be more in line with its historical practices. This approach could be initiated while the new niche market is researched.

Educational Objective 3

3-1. Insurers adjust pricing to respond to the different levels of risk within a portfolio in a three-step process:

a. They subdivide the line into smaller, homogeneous groups and use the process of risk classification to adjust rates for each group.

b. They analyze the unique loss experience for each rate class.

c. They adjust rates to reflect the relatively higher or lower loss exposure of each rate class by applying rate relativity factors.

3-2. The calculation of a base rate for an insurance class or product assumes uniformity in loss frequency and severity. In reality, however, the frequency and severity of losses and the cost of claim settlements within a portfolio can vary significantly. For example, the potential severity of a fire loss is greater for a home located in a remote area.

3-3. The insurer could add roofs ten and fifteen years of age as relativity factors. Additionally, the insurer might add windstorm-prone territories as relativity factors. These relativities will be especially important if competitors are already applying them because the insurer might be adversely selected against by offering lower prices than competitors.

Educational Objective 4

4-1. Actuaries typically express loss frequencies as percentages that are calculated for a particular period, such as one year. To identify loss frequency trends, they review several years' worth of loss frequency information and often adjust for any event (such as a catastrophe) that causes a change in loss frequency.

4-2. Loss severity trends refer to the average size losses for a rating class over time.

4-3. An actuary may exclude reserve takedowns from loss severity calculations because large reserve takedowns artificially reduce the loss severity for the year in which the takedown occurs.

4-4. Actuaries use the comparison and analysis of the frequency and severity of losses among different groups so they can use the results as the basis for establishing rate relativity factors.

Educational Objective 5

5-1. To meet regulatory objectives in all states, insurance rates must not be inadequate, excessive, or unfairly discriminatory.

5-2. When evaluating statewide information to determine rate adequacy, actuaries must use caution because some insurers include atypical results, such as those caused by a severe windstorm season, and because statewide information includes premium and loss data for both profitable and unprofitable insurers.

5-3. Regulatory authorities typically prevent insurers from charging unreasonably high rates by requiring that proposed rate changes be filed with statistical evidence that incurred losses and expenses warrant the requested rate change, limiting rate increases and restricting total rate levels regardless of insurers' evidence of needs, and using their authority to roll back rates if necessary.

5-4. The six social objectives that insurers' rates must meet are that they must be affordable, coverage must be available, insurers must provide risk control incentives, rates must be responsive to change, they must provide rate stability, and they must be responsive to controllable rating factors.

5-5. Insurers derive investment profit from investment income, realized capital gains, and unrealized capital gains.

Educational Objective 6

6-1. These answers apply to questions regarding whether a rate adjustment is needed:

a. The actuarial staff would first obtain the losses, premiums, and exposure units for this territory over the last three years. Based on this information, incurred losses are divided by exposure units to arrive at an annual loss cost amount.

b. The relative performance is calculated by dividing the insurer's loss costs by the pooled loss costs ($253/$352 = 71%). The results indicate that the insurer's loss cost of $253 is 71 percent of the pooled loss costs. Actuaries may be concerned that the insurer's loss costs do not track closely with the pooled data. This would indicate that the insurer's results are not credible, reducing the actuaries' confidence in this data.

c. The percentage change in loss severity in the prior year is averaged with the percentage change in the current year to determine the projected change in loss severity for the following year. That projection is the basis for the rate relativity factor for loss severity. In this case, 12 percent is added to 9 percent and then divided by 2, or a 10.5 percent projection. The rate relativity factor is 1.105.

Direct Your Learning 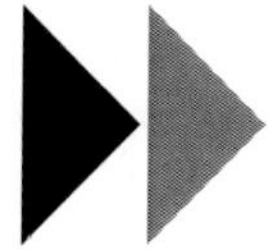

11

Personal Lines Portfolio Management

Educational Objectives

After learning the content of this assignment, you should be able to:

1. Apply analysis tools and approaches used in personal lines portfolio management to determine the root cause of results that do not meet goals.
2. Explain how changes in key indicators and the risk profile for a portfolio are analyzed and corrected.
3. Given a case regarding a personal lines portfolio that is not meeting its loss ratio goals, apply the reunderwriting process to bring the portfolio within goals.
4. Evaluate methods of improving portfolio management.
5. Given a case study regarding a personal lines portfolio that is not meeting its goals, formulate actions that will improve underwriting profitability.

Outline

- **Portfolio Management Analysis Tools and Approaches**
  - A. Making Assumptions and Working With Imperfect Data
  - B. Root Cause Analysis Tools and Approaches
    1. Five Whys
    2. Root Cause Analysis
    3. Common Cause Analysis
  - C. Reunderwriting Tools and Approaches
    1. Investigations Based on Questions
    2. Fix-It-Twice Approach
- **Portfolio Key Indicator Analysis**
  - A. Key Policy Indicators
  - B. Risk Profile Analysis
  - C. Possible Corrective Actions and Their Limitations
    1. Product Changes
    2. Underwriting Changes
    3. Service Changes
    4. Automation Changes
- **Portfolio Reunderwriting Case Study**
  - A. AmberRock Case Facts
  - B. Case Analysis Tools and Information
  - C. Steps in the Reunderwriting Process
    1. Analyzing the Portfolio
    2. Identifying and Distinguishing Problems
    3. Formulating Possible Corrective Actions
    4. Selecting Corrective Actions
    5. Implementing Corrective Actions
    6. Monitoring the Portfolio
- **Evaluating Portfolio Management Methods**
  - A. Credit-Related Underwriting and Pricing
  - B. Modeling
    1. Predictive Models
    2. Catastrophe Modeling
  - C. Outsourcing Data Collection
    1. Information Verification
    2. Subject Matter Experts
    3. External Reports
  - D. Increasing Data Collection
    1. Predictive Variable Information
    2. Rating Variable Information
    3. Underwriting Exception Tracking
- **Personal Lines Portfolio Management/Underwriting Profitability Case Study**
  - A. Case Facts
  - B. Case Analysis Tools
  - C. Case Analysis Steps
    1. Examine Results Compared to Goals
    2. Examine Trends in Results
    3. Formulate Actions
    4. Implement Actions
    5. Monitor Results

Before starting a new assignment, briefly review the Educational Objectives of those preceding it.

For each assignment, you should define or describe each of the Key Words and Phrases and answer each of the Review and Application Questions.

Educational Objective 1

Apply analysis tools and approaches used in personal lines portfolio management to determine the root cause of results that do not meet goals.

Key Words and Phrases

Root cause analysis (RCA)

Reunderwriting

Common cause analysis (CCA)

Event and causal factor chart

Change analysis

Barrier analysis

Review Questions

1-1. List the steps a portfolio manager takes when a portfolio is not meeting policy count or profitability goals.

1-2. Describe the four steps in the Five Whys analysis approach.

1-3. Outline the major steps in root cause analysis.

1-4. Explain how an event and causal factor chart visually depicts a sequence of events.

1-5. Explain how a change analysis seeks to determine the cause of an undesirable event.

1-6. Explain how reunderwriting is a specialized process of root cause analysis.

Application Questions

1-7. Give an example of a problem situation that uses the Five Whys approach to reveal both visible and root causes.

1-8. Analyze the six-month loss results for Insurers Automobile Portfolio to determine how the portfolio is performing relative to its loss results goals, and explain what recommendations, if any, should be made to change product, underwriting, or pricing.

Six-Month Results for Insurers Automobile Portfolio: Loss Results

	Incurred Losses ($000s)	Percentage of Goal	Loss Count	Percentage of Goal	Average Loss
Annual Goals (Monthly goals are an even distribution of annual goals throughout the year.)					
	$6,000		4,800		$1,250
Cumulative YTD Results					
Jan.	$495	99.0%	400	100.0	$1,237
Feb.	$985	98.5%	750	93.7	$1,400
March	$1,465	97.6%	1,125	93.7	$1,280
Apr.	$1,975	98.7%	1,535	95.9	$1,243
May	$2,475	99.0%	1,925	96.2	$1,100
June	$2,970	99.0%	2,330	97.0	$1,222

Educational Objective 2

Explain how changes in key indicators and the risk profile for a portfolio are analyzed and corrected.

Review Questions

2-1. What is a portfolio manager?

2-2. What are three key indicators used to measure the performance of a portfolio of insurance policies?

2-3. What is a risk profile analysis?

2-4. Describe four actions an insurer can take to make insurance policies more attractive to customers.

Application Questions

2-5. If you were the portfolio manager reviewing the homeowners policy retention data, what questions would it raise, and what would you do to answer them?

Year	Retention Percentage
2004	80
2005	80
2006	80
2007	81
2008	83
2009	84
2010	85

2-6. If you were the portfolio manager reviewing selected loss data for a portfolio of homeowners policies, what questions would you ask, and how would you arrange to answer them?

Six-Months Loss Results for Homeowners Portfolio

	Average Loss	Loss Ratio
January	$2,000	72%
February	$2,200	73%
March	$2,300	73%
April	$2,400	74%
May	$2,500	75%
June	$2,500	75%

Educational Objective 3

Given a case regarding a personal lines portfolio that is not meeting its loss ratio goals, apply the reunderwriting process to bring the portfolio within goals.

Application Question

3-1. Auto Insurance Company's (AIC) six-month portfolio report shows that premiums are roughly on target, the policies in force (PIF) and the new policy count are meeting the established annual goals, and new policies meet underwriting guidelines. However, losses incurred in the six-month period are far above those predicted.

A causes-of-loss summary indicates increased auto theft and vandalism losses only in Territories 3 and 9, where unemployment has escalated rapidly because of a severe recession. Additionally, these two mixed light-industrial and residential territories either contain or are near many business closings. A major employer in each of these two territories has closed within the past year, along with many smaller businesses such as restaurants, dry cleaners, and small grocery and liquor stores. Producers report that most residences have no off-street parking, exposing autos to theft and vandalism. A report of theft and vandalism losses indicates that many of the losses have been perpetrated by teenagers and young adults. Another report indicates an elevated high-school dropout rate in the two territories within the past year, along with an extremely low employment rate for high-school dropouts and recent high-school graduates.

If these trends continue, the loss ratio likely will continue to deteriorate, and the portfolio will be unprofitable. How might AIC's portfolio manager apply the reunderwriting process to solve this problem?

Educational Objective 4

Evaluate methods of improving portfolio management.

Key Words and Phrases

Credit scoring

Modeling

Predictive modeling

Catastrophe model

Review Questions

4-1. Describe the advantages to insurers of using credit-based insurance scores.

4-2. Explain how modeling allows portfolio managers to use technology to improve the underwriting process.

4-3. List the four elements incorporated into catastrophe models used for a personal lines book of business.

4-4. Explain why it is important for insurers to verify information provided by customers on insurance applications.

Application Question

4-5. Monica is a portfolio manager who is reviewing a book of homeowners business. These homeowners policies have been unprofitable over the past year, and Monica is developing a plan of actions to improve profitability for the next year.

How can predictive modeling assist Monica in developing actions to improve the profitability of this book of business?

Educational Objective 5

Given a case study regarding a personal lines portfolio that is not meeting its goals, formulate actions that will improve underwriting profitability.

Application Question

5-1. Ken is a portfolio manager for a large national insurer that specializes in personal lines coverage. He is reviewing a portfolio of homeowners policies written in one of the insurers' regional offices. This book of business has experienced a poor loss ratio for the past two years. Ken is in the process of formulating actions to improve the profitability of this book of business.

a. Identify the three primary determinants of underwriting results.

b. Describe the portfolio management tools available to Ken as he reviews this portfolio.

c. Describe the steps in the reunderwriting process.

Answers to Assignment 11 Questions

NOTE: These answers are provided to give students a basic understanding of acceptable types of responses. They often are not the only valid answers and are not intended to provide an exhaustive response to the questions.

Educational Objective 1

1-1. A portfolio manager takes these steps when a portfolio is not meeting its goals:

- Identify potential causes
- Analyze data to confirm the cause of the problem
- Identify and recommend changes in the product, underwriting, or pricing to assist in meeting the goals

1-2. The Five Whys approach entails these four steps:

- Write down the problem, describing it completely
- Ask why the problem happens and write down the answer under the problem described
- If the written answer doesn't explain the root cause of the problem, ask why again and write down that answer
- Repeat Step 3 until satisfied that the cause has been identified

1-3. Root cause analysis entails these steps:

- Clearly define the undesired outcome
- Gather data, including a list of potential causes
- Continue asking "Why" to identify root causes
- Check logic to eliminate items that are not causes
- Generate solutions that address the visible and root causes

1-4. The event and causal factor chart is a horizontal chart showing the sequence of events leading to a problem and the conditions affecting events. The events and conditions are depicted within symbols to indicate types of events and the influence of the conditions.

1-5. A change analysis compares two similar events, one with the problem occurring, the other without the problem occurring. The comparison looks for any differences, however slight they may be, to see whether the differences may have caused the problem.

1-6. Reunderwriting looks at the underperformance of a portfolio as an undesirable event and analyzes data to identify the cause of the underperformance. It then determines and recommends changes to product, underwriting, or pricing to help the portfolio achieve the policy count and profitability goals.

1-7. The example should state the problem and have at least four or five questions of "Why?" and an answer written for each why, as in this example:

Problem: An unusually high number of auto insurance policyholders in a geographic territory are not renewing their policies.

- Why are policyholders not renewing? Because they had to wait two weeks for action on an auto claim because the claim representative staff had to handle a higher than usual number of claims because of multiple hailstorms in a one-month period.
- Why didn't the claim representative staff request additional adjuster help from adjacent territories to reduce the waiting time? They did, but adjacent available staff were in short supply and could not provide any help.
- Why were claim representative staff in short supply? Because the adjacent territory staff had been assigned to special duty in a more distant territory to respond to a serious and widespread catastrophe.
- Why weren't other claim support personnel quickly trained to handle simple auto claims and assigned to such claims? Because no training material had been prepared.
- Why was there no prepared training? Because no one had foreseen the need for or the possibility of using claim support personnel in a limited role.

1-8. Incurred losses are running slightly below target (99.0%), loss count is running slightly below target (97.0%), and monthly average losses are running around the target of $1,250, with only February being significantly above the target average loss. Because the portfolio is performing close to loss goals, no change is recommended on the basis of loss results. Note: The portfolio manager may uncover other performance issues when looking at other key indicators, such as policies in force.

Educational Objective 2

2-1. A portfolio manager is an insurer's employee responsible for achieving the premium, loss ratio, and product-mix goals for a subset of all insurance policies written by the insurer.

2-2. These are the key indicators:

- Policies in force
- New policy count
- Policy retention

2-3. A risk profile analysis is a careful examination of key policy characteristics at specific times or for specific time periods done to uncover key relationships between policy characteristics.

2-4. These are four insurer actions:

- Make contract changes to extend coverage or offer new coverage
- Offer new service features that other insurers do not
- Change underwriting criteria so guidelines are less restrictive
- Automate the policy application process for faster application and acceptance

2-5. When reviewing the homeowners policy retention data, a portfolio manager would encounter these questions to be answered:

- How does this growing increase in retention compare with industry-wide average percentages? Compare with industry average data.
- How much does the retention percentage vary by state? Compare with industry averages by state.
- How much does the retention percentage vary by territory within the insurer's portfolio? Break down the retention percentage by territory.
- Why is the retention rate rising? Look for explanations such as the exit of insurers from the market or expanded coverages or services in the product line; conduct policyholder surveys.

2-6. Losses are increasing. Ask for claim data by cause of loss, type of property, and territory. Consider other policy data if these data do not reveal possible differences or causes.

Educational Objective 3

3-1. A loss severity problem indicates pricing inadequacy. AIC's portfolio manager should examine losses that have occurred in the last six months and the associated loss exposures to identify the reasons for the unexpected losses and to take action. The portfolio manager can decide to apply the Five Whys analysis to this problem.

The first question is, "Why is the loss ratio suddenly deteriorating?" The increased auto theft and vandalism losses in Territories 3 and 9 appear to provide the answer to this question.

The portfolio manager then asks, "Why are these concentrations of losses occurring?" and, along with that question, "Why are these concentrations of losses occurring in these territories?'" The report that unemployment has escalated, along with the closing of many businesses, and the street parking of residents' autos might answer these questions. Additionally, the elevated high-school dropout rate and lack of opportunity for dropouts and recent graduates further contribute to the theft and vandalism losses.

The next "why" question is "Why are these losses that seem to be related to economic hardships occurring in only two territories?" That many businesses have closed, including major employers, in those two territories can answer this question.

The next "why" question the portfolio manager will ask is, "Why has the closing of employers in Territories 3 and 9 caused an increase in losses?" This community has serious economic problems with unemployment and juvenile delinquency.

AIC's portfolio manager decides to raise premiums significantly to cover the increased loss exposures of auto theft and vandalism. The portfolio manager must expedite actions that require state filings for rate increases, and AIC must notify policyholders of the increase upon their next renewals. After the increased rates have been implemented, the portfolio manager must continue to carefully monitor the success of the rate increase and must scrutinize other territories for similar trends in what may become a generally deteriorating economic climate in a broader area.

In summary, reunderwriting involves these steps: analyzing the portfolio to identify and distinguish problems; formulating, selecting, and implementing corrective actions; and monitoring the portfolio.

Educational Objective 4

4-1. The use of credit-based insurance scores provides these advantages for insurers:

- Credit-based insurance scores allow insurers to improve rating methodologies and to develop premiums that are commensurate with expected loss levels.
- Insurers can use credit-based insurance scores to target existing customers who have lower loss potential to improve account retention and overall profitability.

4-2. Portfolio managers use various hypothetical models to project future loss levels, the frequency or severity of catastrophes, and required pricing.

4-3. Catastrophe models for a personal lines book of business incorporate these elements:

- Geographic location
- Type of catastrophe
- Exposure information
- Replacement cost estimates

4-4. It is important for insurers to verify information provided by customers on insurance applications because if application information is inaccurate, then the selection and pricing decisions based on the information will also be incorrect and could result in poor underwriting results.

4-5. Predictive modeling can be used to determine future losses and profitability for these homeowners policies. Monica can examine specific variables to project future results. Such variables would include construction type, age of the home, public protection class, cause of loss, and territory. Based on the results of her analysis, changes could be made in eligibility requirements or pricing to improve the profitability of this book of business.

Educational Objective 5

5-1. These answers apply to improving the profitability of a book of business:

a. The three primary determinants of underwriting results are these:

- Increasing premiums
- Decreasing losses
- Reducing expenses

b. Ken will use tools such as making assumptions and working with imperfect data, root cause analysis, and reunderwriting.

c. The reunderwriting process involves analyzing the homeowners book of business to identify the cause of the increase in losses, identifying and distinguishing the underlying causes that might affect the entire portfolio, and selecting the best corrective action to improve profitability. Ken will then implement these corrective actions and monitor the portfolio to assess the effectiveness of the changes in improving its profitability.

Exam Information

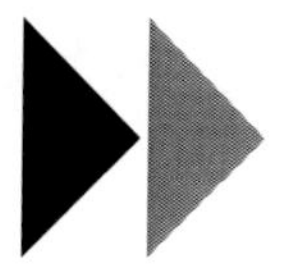

About Institutes Exams

Exam questions are based on the Educational Objectives stated in the course guide and textbook. The exam is designed to measure whether you have met those Educational Objectives. The exam does not necessarily test every Educational Objective. It tests over a balanced sample of Educational Objectives.

How to Prepare for Institutes Exams

What can you do to prepare for an Institutes exam? Students who pass Institutes exams do the following:

- Use the assigned study materials. Focus your study on the Educational Objectives presented at the beginning of each course guide assignment. Thoroughly read the textbook and any other assigned materials, and then complete the course guide exercises. Choose a study method that best suits your needs; for example, participate in a traditional class, online class, or informal study group; or study on your own. Use The Institutes' SMART Study Aids (if available) for practice and review. If this course has an associated SMART Online Practice Exams product, you will find an access code on the inside back cover of this course guide. This access code allows you to print a full practice exam and to take additional online practice exams that will simulate an actual credentialing exam.
- Become familiar with the types of test questions asked on the exam. The practice exam in this course guide or in the SMART Online Practice Exams product will help you understand the different types of questions you will encounter on the exam.
- Maximize your test-taking time. Successful students use the sample exam in the course guide or in the SMART Online Practice Exams product to practice pacing themselves. Learning how to manage your time during the exam ensures that you will complete all of the test questions in the time allotted.

Types of Exam Questions

The exam for this course consists of objective questions of several types.

The Correct-Answer Type

In this type of question, the question stem is followed by four responses, one of which is absolutely correct. Select the *correct* answer.

Which one of the following persons evaluates requests for insurance to determine which applicants are accepted and which are rejected?

a. The premium auditor

b. The loss control representative

c. The underwriter

d. The risk manager

The Best-Answer Type

In this type of question, the question stem is followed by four responses, only one of which is best, given the statement made or facts provided in the stem. Select the *best* answer.

Several people within an insurer might be involved in determining whether an applicant for insurance is accepted. Which one of the following positions is primarily responsible for determining whether an applicant for insurance is accepted?

a. The loss control representative

b. The customer service representative

c. The underwriter

d. The premium auditor

The Incomplete-Statement or Sentence-Completion Type

In this type of question, the last part of the question stem consists of a portion of a statement rather than a direct question. Select the phrase that *correctly* or *best* completes the sentence.

Residual market plans designed for individuals who are unable to obtain insurance on their personal property in the voluntary market are called

a. VIN plans.

b. Self-insured retention plans.

c. Premium discount plans.

d. FAIR plans.

"All of the Above" Type

In this type of question, only one of the first three answers could be correct, or all three might be correct, in which case the best answer would be "All of the above." Read all the answers and select the *best* answer.

When a large commercial insured's policy is up for renewal, who is likely to provide input to the renewal decision process?

a. The underwriter

b. The loss control representative

c. The producer

d. All of the above

"All of the following, EXCEPT:" Type

In this type of question, responses include three correct answers and one answer that is incorrect or is clearly the least correct. Select the *incorrect* or *least correct* answer.

All of the following adjust insurance claims, EXCEPT:

a. Insurer claims representatives

b. Premium auditors

c. Producers

d. Independent adjusters

About the Code of Professional Conduct

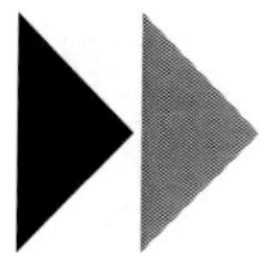

This is a brief summary of information appearing in greater detail in the CPCU Code of Professional Conduct.

All CPCU candidates and CPCUs are bound by the CPCU Code of Professional Conduct. The Code describes both high goals and minimum standards of conduct.

- The high goals described in the Canons challenge all CPCUs and CPCU candidates to aspire to the highest level of ethical performance in all of their professional activities.
- The minimum standards of conduct, described in the Rules, maintain the integrity of the CPCU designation. CPCUs and CPCU candidates are obligated to at least meet the minimum standards in the Rules, and failure to do so may subject a CPCU—or a CPCU candidate—to disciplinary measures.

In the process of satisfying the ethics requirement, CPCU candidates study the Code and are tested to ensure that all CPCUs understand their ethical obligations. The ultimate goal of the Code is to foster highly ethical conduct on the part of all CPCUs.

The CPCU Code of Professional Conduct Canons

Canon 1—Insurance professionals should endeavor to place the public interest above their own.

Canon 2—Insurance professionals should seek continually to maintain and improve their professional knowledge, skills, and competence.

Canon 3—Insurance professionals should obey all laws and regulations, and should avoid any conduct or activity that would cause unjust harm to others.

Canon 4—Insurance professionals should be diligent in the performance of their occupational duties and should continually strive to improve the functioning of the insurance mechanism.

Canon 5—Insurance professionals should aspire to raise the professional and ethical standards in the insurance business.

Canon 6—Insurance professionals should strive to establish and maintain dignified and honorable relationships with those whom they serve, with fellow insurance practitioners, and with members of other professions.

Canon 7—Insurance professionals should assist in improving the public understanding of insurance and risk management.

Canon 8—CPCUs should honor the integrity of the CPCU designation and respect the limitations placed on its use.

Canon 9—CPCUs should assist in maintaining the integrity of the CPCU Code of Professional Conduct.